The Hist

by
Henry S. Beebe

The History Of Perus
by Henry S. Beebe

Copyright © 2024

All Rights reserved.

No part of this publication may be reproduced, stored in a retrieval system, or transmitted in any form or by any means, electronic, mechanical, photocopying or Otherwise, without the written permission of the publisher.
The author/editor asserts the moral right to be identified as the author/editor of this work.

ISBN: 978-93-62762-17-7

Published by
DOUBLE 9 BOOKS
2/13-B, Ansari Road
Daryaganj, New Delhi – 110002
info@double9books.com
www.double9books.com
Tel. 011-40042856

This book is under public domain

ABOUT THE AUTHOR

Henry S. Beebe, a distinguished historian and scholar, is celebrated for his magnum opus, "The History of Peru." This comprehensive work offers a meticulous and insightful examination of Peru's rich and complex past, spanning from ancient civilizations to contemporary society. Beebe's masterful narrative skillfully traces the country's historical trajectory, exploring its cultural, political, and socio-economic developments with meticulous detail and scholarly rigor. Through engaging prose and extensive research, Beebe brings to life the diverse peoples, events, and movements that have shaped Peru's identity and contributed to its unique cultural heritage. From the rise and fall of indigenous civilizations to the colonial era, independence struggle, and modern challenges, Beebe provides readers with a comprehensive understanding of Peru's historical significance within the broader context of Latin American history. "The History of Peru" stands as a testament to Beebe's expertise as a historian and his dedication to illuminating the complexities of the past. It serves as an indispensable resource for scholars, students, and anyone interested in delving into the fascinating history of this vibrant South American nation.

CONTENTS

INTRODUCTORY 7
CHAPTER I 9
CHAPTER II 12
CHAPTER III 16
CHAPTER IV 19
CHAPTER V 21
CHAPTER VI 23
CHAPTER VII 25
CHAPTER VIII 29
CHAPTER IX 32
CHAPTER X 37
CHAPTER XI 47
CHAPTER XII 57

INTRODUCTORY

It can hardly be said that a town of a population of three thousand six hundred and fifty-two souls, dating back but about twenty years to its first rude tenement and solitary family, can have any history. The events of any public interest are so few, and their importance so small, that no reasonable hope can be entertained that their recital will be any thing but a matter of indifference to others than the present or former residents, or those connected with them by ties of consanguinity, or having an interest in its advancement and prosperity. It is true that at some future time, the record may be useful to the historian, if it should be so fortunate as to survive. The statistics have been collected with care and considerable labor, and are believed to be correct and reliable. Beyond this the writer claims no merit for the work. The anecdotes and events related, not strictly statistical, have all transpired under his personal observation and knowledge, during a residence dating back to the embryo town.

Most persons who have had the temerity to undertake the relation of cotemporary events, and to speak of cotemporary actors, have received more kicks than coppers for their pains. How far the writer will escape their general fate remains to be seen. Knowing the dangerous ground whereon he was treading, he has endeavored to confine himself to the simple relation of undisputed facts, abstaining from all comments and speculation thereon. He has not set himself up as a public censor or a public eulogist. It is not to be supposed that he has been without partisan and prejudiced views of public questions. These he has endeavored to suppress and to "render unto Cæsar the things which are Cæsars." Nor has he undertaken to draw a rose colored picture for the benefit of Eastern Capitalists, or those seeking a home in the west—to throw bait to Gudgeons.—In fact, it will be admitted, that his picture is of the soberest and dullest kind of grey. Would that it could be here and there touched with lighter and more cheerful hues; but truth is inexorable, and demands the strictest loyalty from those who worship at her shrine.

The people of Peru may be a little curious to know why a person, whose pursuits in life have been hitherto very far removed from those of a writer for the public eye, should have undertaken a task for which previous practice and experience have so little qualified him. He begs to assure them that it was entirely an accident—no literary ambition prompted him at all. To be sure he had heard that

> "'Tis pleasant sure to see one's name in print,
> And a book's a book although there's nothing in't,"

but that was not it. Having a little leisure, he had undertaken to gather and condense some statistics of the town for the publisher of a Directory of La Salle County. Having commenced the task he became interested therein, and extended his researches and remarks to a length quite too formidable for their original purpose. But he resolved not to hide his light under a bushel—hence the present infliction which he hopes will be borne with commendable fortitude.

CHAPTER I

The City of Peru is situated in the Westerly part of La Salle County, Illinois, on the Northern bank of the Illinois River, at the head of Navigation, and at the Junction of the Illinois and Michigan Canal. Distance from Chicago 100 miles, and from Saint Louis 230. The territory embraced within the corporated limits, is Sec. 16 and 17, and all those fractional parts of 20 and 21, which lie north of the river, Town 33, Range 1, East of the Third Principal Meridian, comprising an area of 1462 Acres.

The settlement of the site occupied by this City was commenced in the Spring of 1836, shortly after the passage of the act incorporating the Illinois and Michigan Central, which was to terminate at or near the mouth of the Little Vermilion, on land owned by the State. It was probably the most eligible site on lands owned by individuals. The Southwest quarter of Sec. 16 was laid out and sold by the School Commissioners in 1834, and called Peru. Ninawa Addition, located on the South East quarter of Sec. 17, and the North East fractional part of 20, upon which the most business part of Peru is at present situated, was owned originally by Lyman D. Brewster, who died in the fall of 1835. It was plated and recorded in 1836, by Theron D. Brewster, at present a leading and influential citizen.

In 1835 the only residents of that portion of territory now occupied by the cities of Peru and La Salle were Lyman D. Brewster, his nephew T. D. Brewster, John Hays and family, Peltiah and Calvin Brewster, Samuel Lapsley and Burton Ayres. In the Spring of 1835, the first building—a store—was erected in Peru by Ulysses Spaulding and H. L. Kinney, late of Central American notoriety. On the 4th July 1836, the first shovel full of earth was excavated upon the Canal. No considerable population was attracted to the town until 1837. Among the people who made this place their home in that and the following years, were Wm. Richardson, J. P. Judson, S. Lisle Smith and his brother Doctor Smith, Fletcher Webster, Daniel Townsend, P. Hall, James Mulford, James Myers, Wm. and Chas. Dresser, Harvey Wood, N. B. Bullock, Jesse Pugsley, Ezra McKinzie, Nathaniel and Isaac Abraham, J. P. Thompson, John Hoffman, C. H. Charles, Asa Mann, Lucius Rumrill, Cornelius Cahill, Cornelius Cokeley, David Dana, Zimri Lewis, Daniel McGin, S. W. Raymond, Geo. B. Martin, Wm. H. Davis, Geo. W. Holley,

Geo. Low, M. Mott, F. Lebeau, A. Hyatt, Ward B. Burnett, O. C. Motley, Wm. Paul, H. P. Woodworth, H. S. Beebe, Harvey Leonard, &c.

At the Session of the Legislature of 1836, the Internal Improvement act was passed, incorporating the Central Rail Road, which was subsequently located upon the same general route as is followed by the present Illinois Central Rail Road, crossing the river at Peru. Operations were commenced on both sides of the river in 1838. During this season very extensive improvements were made, large accessions of population took place, and the settlement began to assume the appearance of a town. In 1839 the whole country was on the top wave of prosperity. Large forces were employed upon both the Canal and Rail Road—numerous other works being contemplated, all terminating at Peru, of course—and the disbursements were large. The town shared the general prosperity. In this year H. P. Woodworth was elected [Transcriber's Note: Error, he was defeated, see the Errata] to the Legislature from La Salle County, which then embraced the present territory of Kendall and Grundy, receiving in Peru 528 votes, being the largest vote ever polled in the precinct, before or since.

On the 6th of December 1838 the inhabitants assembled at the tavern of Zimri Lewis, and organised a meeting by the appointment of H. S. Beebe, Chairman, and J. B. Judson, Secretary, and voted to take the preliminary steps for organizing the town as a borough under the general Incorporation Act. At a census taken the same month there were found to be within the limits proposed to be embraced in the Borough, to wit: The South half of Section 16, the South East quarter of Section 17, and all that part of Section 20 lying North of the river—about one square mile.

Males over 21 years of age	175
Females and minors	251
Total	426

On the 15th of December an election was held to decide upon such organization with the following result.

For organization	40
Against organization	1

On the same day an election was held for Trustees which resulted in the election of M. Mott, F. Lebeau, C. H. Charles, Z. Lewis and O. C. Motley. The Board elected Z. Lewis, President; T. D. Brewster, Clerk; Z. Lewis, jr. Constable; and James Myers, Assessor. On the 1st of April 1839, O. C. Motley resigned and H. P. Woodworth was elected in his place. D. J. Townsend was afterwards appointed Street Commissioner.

The first religious meeting assembled in the locality was held in the early part of this year, in a log shanty, in the western part of the town. This meeting was attended by about a dozen young reprobates who concerted, that if the preacher should confine himself to what they should judge to be the "appropriate sphere of his duties," should preach piety and righteousness in the abstract without making any particular application thereof, or rebuking any particular practice cherished by these self constituted censors, and should abstain from all offensive personal or local allusions, the most decorous propriety was to be observed. But if, on the contrary, he should see fit to indulge in any reproof of evil practices which they were conscious the community had credit for, whether justly or not, the indignity was to be instantly resented. In pursuance of this concert they repaired to the place of worship, each provided with a tobacco pipe well filled, and a match. During the preliminary exercises and a portion of the sermon the most respectful attention and devout bearing were manifested; but when the preacher unfortunately indulged in illusions, believed by these censors to be intended to have a direct local application, a rap on the bench was made as a signal by the leader, and instantly twelve matches were struck and twelve pipes lighted. No smile was seen and no word was spoken; but twelve sedate and imperturbable smokers tugged vigorously at their pipes. The room was soon filled with the smoke and aroma; and after a few attempts at rebuke, ejaculated between stifled spasms of coughing, the preacher incontinently left; but not without making a stand at the door, where a few comparatively pure respirations were obtained, and hurling back some rather unchristian anathemas upon the graceless and sacrilegious scamps, whose scandalous conduct had so unceremoniously put him to flight, and upon the people by whom they were tolerated. Of course, "the better part of community" set the seal of their disapprobation upon such disreputable and disorderly proceedings.

CHAPTER II

At an election held on the 19th December 1839 H. P. Woodworth, Simon Kinney, Z. Burnham, C. H. Charles, and Isaac Abraham were elected Trustees. Whole number of votes polled 40.

The Board elected Simon Kinney, President; M. Mott, Collector; T. D. Brewster, Treasurer; and Walter Meriman, Clerk. In the course of the year Kinney resigned as Trustee and Meriman as Clerk, and Cornelius Cahill and James Bradford were elected to fill their respective places. The places of Burnham and Charles became vacant by death, and Ezra McKinzie and Churchill Coffing were elected to fill them. In 1840 came the grand financial collapse. The foreign capitalists refused to lend us any more money. The later residents of Illinois can scarcely comprehend the condition of things which preceded and ensued. By the Internal Improvement Act, which puts all Congressional omnibus bills entirely into the shade, a system of Rail Roads was to be commenced simultaneously in all parts of the State, running in all manner of directions, through regions scarcely explored; and counties which were not fortunate enough to lie in the direction of any place, and thus not to be traversed by Rail Roads, were bribed into the support of the bill by distributions of money, all to be borrowed on the faith of the State. Other acts were passed authorizing loans for prisons, hospitals, asylums and State Houses. At the same time the Canal was being prosecuted on State credit. Counties followed the example of the State by borrowing money to build Court Houses, Jails &c. But at length the bottom fell out of the whole concern. Unknown Millions had been squandered and not one public undertaking was completed. Public and private credit were annihilated. Northern Illinois produced nothing for exportation, and every kind of business was dependent upon the disbursements on the public works. The State, Counties, Towns, Banks, corporations and individuals were alike bankrupt. No gleam of light shone in the future. Repudiation, public and private, appeared to be the only alternative. Even the vampires who had been gorged upon the treasury were overwhelmed in the general avalanche. The few who had hoarded and possessed the means, left the State; and emigration for years avoided it as though it had been one great hospital of lepers.

No place experienced the general prostration more sensibly than Peru. The writer of this with a family to support, did not possess in the year 1841 in the aggregate, a sum of money equal to five dollars. Letters lay in the Post Office from the inability of those to whom they were addressed to pay the postage. Nor was this embarrassment confined to individuals.—Gov. Ford once told the writer, that he had been compelled to allow letters, directed to him upon official business, to remain in the Federal Post Office, his own means or credit, or that of the Sovereign State of Illinois being insufficient to raise the embargo. Property of no kind had any apparent value whatever. The town gradually lost its inhabitants, until in 1842, probably not over two hundred souls remained. These were mainly the less fortunate portion who could not get away. One Store, a Drug Shop, the Post Office, and two Taverns were the only places that remained open to the public. Society existed upon a truly republican basis. No envy was excited in the breasts of the humble and poor by the brilliant equipages and establishments of the rich. The creditor who would have seriously asked payment of his debtor would have been saluted with one universal shout of derision.—As well might he have asked the sea to give up its dead. His money was gone to that bourne whence "nary red" would ever return. It was seriously proposed to enact a law making every man's note a tender for debts—always excepting the notes of the creditor himself. This condition of things produced a state of society never witnessed by the writer, before or since. The prevailing influence was so universal and complete as to reduce all to a common level. A sympathy and community of feeling pervaded all Illinois humanity. Thanks to a prolific soil and sparse population, nobody was in danger of starvation.

The following incident illustrates the scarcity and value of money about this time. The only merchants who pretended to keep their stores open for business, and were able to replenish their stock, were the brothers A. one of them at present an estimable and valued citizen, and the other a worthy farmer living in the neighborhood. Money was scarce wherewith to pay freights, and the only resource was to transport wheat, taken of the farmers for debts, to Chicago, a distance of one hundred miles, where it was worth about fifty cents per bushel. One of the persons employed in the transportation was a farmer named M.—One of the brothers and the writer accompanied the teams. After the wheat had been marketed and unloaded, M. with a very grave and serious face, desired a private conference with A. Taking him a little apart from the writer, and speaking in a voice loud enough to be distinctly overheard, he informed him that he was under the necessity of asking him for some money. A. started as if a snake had stung him. He expressed surprise at such a sudden call, under the circumstances, and reminded M. of the exertions and sacrifices which he had been compelled to make to raise money for charges, and that withal he had but barely enough for that purpose; and concluded by hoping that his demands would be extremely limited. M. replied that they would be no more extensive than his necessities absolutely required, and he thought about "two bits would do him." This announcement greatly relieved A. who immediately responded to the demand. When it is understood, that the almost universal practice in traveling, at that time, was to "camp out," the commissary department drawing its supplies from the domestic larder and corn crib, it will be perceived that "two bits" would go a good way in eking out the stores and supplying any deficiency.

Another incident occurred about this time which also illustrates, in some degree, the spirit of the times. Two citizens who shall be named B. and M. had been in the habit of bantering each other about their poverty. M. persisted in assuming that he was not as poor as B., and that it was all owing to his superior address and financial ability. This ridiculous assumption may be understood, when it is stated that neither party could, from every available resource, have raised a sum in money equal to the present price of a barrel of flour. M. complained to B. about his hogs running at large, and threatened that if they were permitted to annoy him he would shut them up and kill them. It so happened that B. did not own a hog in the world—a fact which he was careful not to disclose. M. commenced to put his threat in execution by building an enclosure in which he incarcerated all vagrant hogs, and proceeded to put them in a condition for slaughtering by a liberal appliance of corn and swill. These things did not escape the observation of B. who waited patiently until the hogs were in a nice condition, when he called upon M. and rather angrily remonstrated with him upon committing so unneighborly an act as to secrete his hogs, alleging that he had searched diligently for them, and that great apprehensions had existed, lest his family might seriously suffer for the want thereof. He reminded him of the cordiality and good feeling which had previously existed between them, of their good natured jokes and banters, and of the general felicity which they had enjoyed in each other's society; and read him a homily upon the advantages to be derived from the practice of honesty and integrity. He insisted, however, upon the unconditional liberation of four particularly promising specimens of the genus, porker. To this M. demurred.—While he admitted that what B. had taken so much pains to remind him of, was in the main true, he urged that the corn wherewith he had fed the hogs was difficult to be obtained, that he had spent much time in feeding and taking care of them, and that it was not right for one man to take advantage of another's wrong act for his own benefit. These arguments somewhat mollified B. who finally agreed to a compromise by which M. was to continue feeding the hogs for a specified time, and then kill and dress them, and bring the carcasses of the two best to the house of B. This compact was carried into effect in good faith. Shortly afterwards B. disclosed the history of this little operation which came to the ears of M. It is confidently believed that he never afterwards boasted of his peculiar gifts of finesse. It is but fair to say, that the real owner of the hogs who had no share in the spoils, pocketed his loss with admirable grace.

In the course of the year 1839 the first newspaper published in Peru, was established by Ford, now Editor and proprietor of the "Lacon Gazette" in connection with Geo. W. Holley who acted as editor, and was called the "Ninawa Gazette." Mr. Holley was a gentleman of considerable literary reputation and made a paper which was eagerly sought for. His writings were principally distinguished for their peculiar vein of humor and pleasantry. The paper was continued until 1841, when the press and materials were removed to Lacon.

The first Church built in the town, was erected by the Methodists in the fall of 1838.

CHAPTER III

At an election held on the 18th December 1840, H. P. Woodworth, Churchill Coffing, Ezra McKinzie, Isaac Abraham and Geo. Low were elected Trustees. Whole number of votes polled 32. This Board elected Isaac Abraham their President; James Bradford Clerk; James Myers, Assessor; F. Lebeau Constable, T. D. Brewster Treasurer; and M. Mott, Street Commissioner. Subsequently F. Mills was elected Constable in place of Lebeau who resigned, and John Hoffman Fire Warden.

On the 27th February 1841 an act passed the Legislature chartering the La Salle and Dixon Rail Road, giving to the Corporation created, the right of way and materials belonging to that part of the old Central Rail Road lying between the two points named. During the year operations were recommenced on this work, and a Bank of issue, pretended to be authorized by the Charter, was opened in La Salle. These operations for a short time galvanized into life the prostrated energies of the remaining inhabitants of Peru, but were shortly succeeded by the bursting of the whole concern. The leading spirit of this movement was a man named A. H. Bangs, who succeeded in making dupes or accomplices of several leading and influential inhabitants of La Salle and Lee Counties. After the explosion it was found that he was a mere adventurer, without character, reputation, capital or credit. Not an hundred dollars in cash or a dollar of good and reliable paper had been used in starting and continuing the construction of forty miles of Rail Road, and putting into operation a Bank which soon flooded the whole country with its worthless promises to pay, and draw liberally upon its imaginary eastern and foreign correspondents. The contractors were, of course, unable to pay the laborers, and the farmers who had supplied them with provisions. The former, enraged by their wrongs, attempted to wreak their vengeance upon the person of the culprit, Bangs. They seized and dragged him through the muddy streets of the town. He was finally rescued by the citizens, partly through menaces and partly through intercession, without material injury, placed in a skiff, and sent down the river. Had he possessed one thousand dollars in real cash, there is not a doubt but that he would have been able to finish and put in operation the road, and to have gone on swimmingly with his Bank for years; such was the confidence, and it might be added, reverence, which a real "capitalist" would at that time have inspired. The relapse was, if possible, more depressing than the former experience.

During this year the second Church—a small but substantial stone edifice, at present occupied by the Episcopal Society—was erected by the liberality of T. D. Brewster, Esq., for the Congregationalist Society. For the use of the Society worshiping in this building, a valuable bell was donated by the late John C. Coffing of Salisbury, Connecticut, father of our distinguished townsman, Hon. Churchill Coffing.

In the summer Mr. Van Buren, then lately retired from the Presidency, accompanied by James K. Paulding then late Secretary of the Navy, made a tour through the western States, and was everywhere received with an ovation.—A Committee was appointed in Peru to receive and escort them to Ottawa. There was then residing here a young man, a carpenter by trade and a great wag, rejoicing in the name America Jones. There also lived here a "Doctor" Harrison, more famous for his effrontery and obtrusive declamation than for his medical learning or skill. He came armed with a diploma or certificate from the Berrien County, Michigan, Medical Society, signed "E. Winslow, President." His attainments and accomplishments were by no means confined to the healing and dissecting art, according to his own persistent declaration. They embraced the grand encyclopedia of science. He was a pugilist, and boasted of many a hard earned field; he was an advocate of the dueling code, and understood precisely the etiquette of the field of Honor, and was ready, should anybody knock a chip from his shoulder, to put in practice the theory which he so eloquently expounded, although it is believed that he never absolutely asserted that his chivalry had been put to the test; he was a musician and an expert at games, particularly "seven up" and "poker;" and he was a military gentleman. He has since attained the rank of Major General, in the service of the State of Michigan. With this brilliant array of accomplishments he naturally attracted the attention of the community, and what was more to the purpose, obtained a very lucrative practice. He numbered among his admirers people in all grades of society. Most zealous among these was a gentleman—an eminent civil engineer—of a high professional and social position. America Jones, above mentioned, concocted a scheme very well calculated to cure him of his extraordinary devotion to the Doctor, and confidence in his professions; and at the same time to indulge his own innate propensity for fun, at the expense of the engineer and another prominent citizen—a lawyer—at present resident. Jones became suddenly very efficient and "numerous" at a meeting called to make arrangements for the reception of the distinguished visitors, although it was probably the first time in his life that he had ever seriously taken part in any thing of the kind, being generally content to look on and distort the action of others into some ludicrous phase. Now Jones had a very clear perception of the Doctor's real merit. He understood instinctively the difference between that and his bombastic pretensions. He knew, too, that his vanity and egotism were only to be adroitly excited, and he would throw himself in a general and continued splurge, in any presence. So he obtained a place for himself and the Doctor on the committee of reception, escort and arrangements. On the trip to Ottawa, he contrived to occupy a carriage in company with the Doctor, the two guests, and the two citizens above referred to. Once on the road, Jones found means to gradually launch the Doctor into the field of general declamation. The latter described the scenery in terms of poetic eulogy; he exhibited his erudition in the early history of the country; he analyzed, in the most scientific manner, the waters of the "Sulphur Springs," and branched off into the abstract laws of chemistry generally; he extemporized an essay upon political economy; he discussed the character of distinguished cotemporary politicians and statesmen; he repeated all the stale newspaper anecdotes and scandal concerning the public men of the day; he asserted his belief that somebody, down on the Mohawk or somewhere else, once wrote a very foolish book, called the "Dutchman's Fireside;" he reviewed and criticised the battles of the Revolution and the naval engagements of the last war with England; he recounted his own exploits and prowess in many a pugilistic encounter; and he indulged in terms of unbounded compliment to, and admiration of the more distinguished portion of his auditory, lamenting that his father had not lived to learn the transcendent honor which had befallen his son, in actually riding in the same carriage with such illustrious personages. These efforts occupied nearly the entire journey to Ottawa, to the unutterable chagrin and annoyance of the two citizens, and the infinite delight and amusement of Jones. How Messrs. Van Buren and Paulding enjoyed the society of the committee is not known.

CHAPTER IV

At an election held on the 11th December 1841, the same Trustees were elected who served the preceding year. Churchill Coffing was elected President; J. Bradford, Clerk; T. D. Brewster, Treasurer and Collector; H. Leonard, Assessor; F. Mills, Constable; H. S. Beebe, Street Commissioner; and J. Hoffman, Fire Warden.

During the year 1842, no event is recollected of sufficient importance to justify a record. The general stagnation continued. Illinois had become as stagnant and inactive as Cathay. People could not be said to live—they merely vegetated.

At an election held on the 15th December 1842, Churchill Coffing, Isaac Abraham, John Hoffman, T. D. Brewster, and H. S. Beebe, were elected Trustees. This Board elected James Bradford, Clerk; S. W. Raymond, Constable; and T. D. Brewster, Treasurer.

On the 21st February, 1843, "An Act to provide for the completion of the Illinois and Michigan Canal, and the payment of the Canal debt" passed the Legislature. Energetic and sagacious measures were at once devised and put into operation for the completion of that great work. To Gov. Ford, Senator Ryan and Col. Oakley, is due the credit of devising the scheme which heralded to the people of Illinois the return of prosperity. This measure was soon followed by gradual improvements in the town. Considerable accessions to its population took place, warehouses and workshops began to be erected, and everything soon assumed the appearance of thrift and progress.

During the season of stagnation, the daily arrival of steamboats from Saint Louis, the debarkation of their passengers, and their departure for Chicago, by Frink, Walker & Co's. coaches, tended more to enliven the town than all other causes combined. This route became a popular one for southern travel, via., the Lakes to New York, particularly during the warmer season; and it was no uncommon thing to witness the departure of from five to ten four-horse post coaches together. The first arrival of a steamboat in the Spring was always hailed as a great event. Two or three months of isolation had sharpened the appetites of the people for intercourse with the great world. The first faint puff, away down among the cotton woods, was caught upon the ear of some anxious and expectant listener, and forthwith the news spread with wonderful celerity throughout the town. All the men and boys gathered upon the landing; all the women and girls upon the hilltops. When the boat hove in sight, conjectures flew thick and fast as to what boat she was; everybody had some theory founded upon the particular manner of her 'scape, the ball upon her jack-staff, the ornaments upon her chimneys, or some other distinguishing mark which each prided himself upon knowing and remembering. When she came within hailing distance, what a hurrah went up from the landing! What a waving of handkerchiefs from the bluffs! Then when her keel fairly grated upon the pebbles of the bank, and a plank was run over her side, what a rush over all her parts! What a shaking of hands all round! What congratulations and welcomes were extended to officers and crew, from captain to firemen! These over, the truth of history extorts the admission, that the space around the bar became the grand rendezvous. A short time spent in this neighborhood by no means tended to lessen the general hilarity and uproar. The news of the arrival of a steamboat soon spread throughout the country. The inhabitants of the interior, inland village of Ottawa, in a very leisurely and dignified way, harnessed up their teams and made a pilgrimage to Peru, on pretence of business, but in point of fact to see a real steamboat.

CHAPTER V

At an election held on the 20th of January, 1843, Churchill Coffing, John R. Merritt, Z. Lewis, Ambrose O'Conner and John Hoffman were elected Trustees. Whole number of votes 92.—This Board elected Churchill Coffing, President; and T. D. Brewster, Treasurer. The revenue arising from taxes on Real Estate was $262.

Peru, from her earliest history, had aspired to become a county seat. Situated upon the extreme western verge of the County of La Salle, she contemplated erecting a new one out of territory to be taken from La Salle, Bureau and Putnam. This scheme was strenuously resisted by Ottawa and the eastern portion of the county. A curtailment on the north and east was cheerfully submitted to, in order to assist in preventing the loss of the western jewel. Much acrimony was engendered by these contests; and all elections for county officers or State Legislature hinged upon this question. The Democratic party was largely in the ascendant; but the schemes of the politicians of that ilk were constantly baffled by the intrusion of this element. The completion of the Canal and Rail Road, furnishing facilities for travel between the two places, mainly put a stop to further agitation.

At an election held on the 25th November, 1844, Churchill Coffing, H. Whitehead, David Dana, Wm. Paul and S. W. Raymond were elected Trustees. Whole number of votes 45. This Board elected H. Whitehead, President; H. S. Beebe, Clerk; J. B. Lovett, Fire Warden; Isaac Abraham, Treasurer; O. C. Parmerly, Street Commissioner; Geo. Low, Collector and Assessor; and E. M. Moore, Constable.

On the 25th February, 1845, an Act passed the Legislature, extending the powers of the Trustees, and providing for their election in the following April.

At an election held on the 7th April, 1845, Churchill Coffing, David Dana, S. W. Raymond, Wm. Paul and H. Whitehead were elected Trustees. Whole number of votes polled 39.

This Board elected Herman Whitehead, President; H. S. Beebe, Clerk; O. C. Parmerly, Street Commissioner; Isaac D. Harmon, Treasurer; George Low, Assessor and Collector; E. M. Moore, Constable; and J. B. Lovett, Fire

Warden. By the death of Moore, the office of Constable soon became vacant, and Z. Lewis, junior, was elected to fill it. The revenue, arising from the tax on Real Estate, was this year $261,-86 cents.

A degree of prosperity had now been attained, little dreamed of three years before. A large trade had gradually grown up and concentrated in Peru. It was no uncommon thing to see wagons loaded with produce, from a distance of sixty, eighty and an hundred miles, seeking a market at this point, and returning loaded with merchandise purchased here. General health, contentment and prosperity prevailed. Stores and dwellings continued to be built, and population to increase.

At an election held on the 6th April, 1846, Jacob S. Beach, Churchill Coffing, William Chumasero, A. M. Thrall and James Cahill were elected Trustees. Whole number of votes 96. This Board elected Churchill Coffing, President; H. S. Beebe, Clerk; George Low, Assessor and Collector; S. W. Raymond, Street Commissioner; I. D. Harmon, Treasurer; David Perry, Constable; and S. N. Maze, Fire Warden. H. F. Killum was subsequently elected Street Commissioner, in place of Raymond who resigned.

In May, another weekly newspaper was established by Nash and Elliott, and called the "Beacon Light." Mr. Nash is the present Clerk of the Circuit Court of La Salle county. The name of this paper was changed to that of "Junction Beacon." It continued about two years under the management of Mead, Higgins and Boyle, either together or successively, and went out.

On the 5th December an ordinance was passed, authorizing the formation of a Hook and Ladder Company, which was the first, last and only attempt to form a Fire Department. The principle effect and probable design of this ordinance was to exempt the members enrolled, from the performance of jury duty. Thirty-five dollars were appropriated for implements; but it is believed that none were ever capable of being brought into use, in cases of emergency, although the town has been devastated since, with many and serious fires.

CHAPTER VI

At an election held on the 5th April, 1847, Churchill Coffing, Wm. Chumasero, Geo. W. Gilson, Joseph P. Turner and Daniel O. Sullivan were elected Trustees. Whole number of votes 63. This Board elected Wm. Chumasero, President; S. W. Raymond, Clerk; James Elliott, Street Commissioner; H. S. Beebe, Treasurer; Geo. Low, Assessor; David Perry, Collector; Joseph P. Turner, Fire Warden; and H. W. Baker, Clerk. Soon after, Raymond resigned and E. S. Holbrook was elected in his place.

The Cemetery, one mile north of the town, was purchased and laid out by this Board.

At an election held in April, 1848, Erasmus Winslow, P. M. Kilduff, I. C. Day, John Morris and S. N. Maze were elected Trustees. Whole number of votes 128. This Board elected Erasmus Winslow, President; David Perry, Clerk; James Elliott, Collector; H. W. Baker, Street Commissioner; F. S. Day, Treasurer; J. P. Thompson, Constable; and Dennis Dunnavan, Fire Warden. Thompson was subsequently elected Street Commissioner, in place of Baker who failed to qualify, and Fire Warden in place of Dunnavan who was removed.

The completion of the Canal, in the Spring of this year, forms an era in the history of the town, and indeed of the State. Its effect upon the town, however, was not so marked and immediate as upon the sister town of La Salle, which then, for the first time, attracted general public attention, and became a formidable rival to her older sister. Upon the latter its favorable effects were more apparent in the course of the two or three following years, when the increased prosperity of the country reacted upon it. The travel, which had always centered at Peru, was mainly diverted to La Salle. Although the waters of the Canal and River were united at Peru, it was soon found, that in consequence of the Steamboat and Canal Boat Basin being at La Salle, the practical junction was there. The forwarding business, after a long and ineffectual struggle on the part of Peru to retain it, finally settled at that point.

In October Holbrook and Underhill established a weekly paper, called the "Peru Telegraph."

The first substantial Stone Ware House built in the town was erected this year, directly upon the river bank, by T. D. Brewster, Esq.

The Spring of 1849 was remarkable for the greatest flood known since the settlement of the country. There had been heavy rains in the month of January which raised the river out of its banks, overflowing all the bottoms. The weather changed to cold suddenly and froze the waters, in many places from bluff to bluff, into a broad crystalline Lake. Such was the case on the bottom above the town, which was covered with a sheet of ice for nearly six miles, to Utica. This mass of intercepted water, together with all the country drained by the head branches of the river, was afterwards covered with a heavy mass of snow. About the first of March the weather again suddenly became warm, and heavy rains set in, which soon loosened the accumulations of snow and ice. Every creek and run contributed a flood, and every ravine and slough a torrent to the swelling river, which on the 9th of March was twenty-five feet, or more, above low water. Its sudden rise loosened the heavy masses of ice spread over the bottoms above, without breaking them up. One of these came down, miles in extent, entirely filling the space between the bluffs, and crushed everything in its course. Trees, indicating a growth of centuries, were as reeds in its path, producing no check to its resistless and majestic motion. The Ware House, heretofore mentioned as being built by Mr. Brewster, then occupied by Brewster and Beebe, was crushed like an egg shell. It was nearly filled with wheat, flour and merchandise, a portion of which had been hastily removed, and a portion was destroyed. The waters soon subsided and the river became very low before the close of navigation in the fall. This was the greatest freshet which has taken place since the settlement of the country by the Whites, but the Indians related to the early settlers accounts of still higher waters. They have asserted that the present site of Ottawa has been submerged within the memory of those now living. Shabone, an Indian well known in Northern Illinois, is reported to have said that he has passed over it in a canoe. In 1844, the great freshet occurred in the Mississippi, raising the waters in the lower part of the Ill. still higher than they afterwards were in 1849. This was not the case with the upper portion of the river. An idea is current in this part of the country, that great freshets recur, continuing throughout the greater portion of the summer, once in seven years. This notion is justified by the recurrence of protracted freshets in 1830, 1837, 1844, 1851 and 1858. Mr. Meginness, in his "Otzinachson" or "History of the West Branch of the Susquehanna," mentions that the same impression prevailed in that region concerning freshets, only that theirs recurred once in fourteen years.

CHAPTER VII

At an election held on the 2d April, 1849, P. M. Kilduff, Frederick Kaiser, S. N. Maze, Noah Sapp and David Lininger were elected Trustees. Whole number of Votes 159. This Board elected P. M. Kilduff, President; Erasmus Winslow, Clerk; Ezra McKinzie, Assessor; James Cahill, Collector; J. P. Thompson, Street Commissioner, Constable and Fire Warden; and H. S. Beebe, Treasurer. In consequence of the absence of Beebe, H. L. Tuller was elected Treasurer in his place.

In the Spring of this year the cholera first made its appearance in the West. In the months of April and May several citizens fell victims to the disease. On the 20th of June it suddenly assumed a malignant and virulent character, and some hundreds were swept off in the course of three or four weeks. The citizens were generally panic stricken, and many fled. It suddenly ceased, and the season thenceforth was healthy.

In the summer of this year the second permanent and substantial warehouse, directly upon the river, was erected by Churchill Coffing, Esq.

At an election held on the 1st April, 1850, T. D. Brewster, I. D. Harmon, William Paul, Erasmus Winslow and William Roush were elected Trustees. Whole number of votes 49—This Board elected William Paul, President; P. M. Kilduff, Clerk; H. L. Tuller, Treasurer; Geo. Low, Assessor; J. P. Thompson, Street Commissioner; Michael Griffith, Constable; Edmund Pennington, Fire Warden; James Cahill, Collector; and Erasmus Winslow, Health Commissioner. During this year the subject of Railroads began to attract the attention of the people of Illinois. The inhabitants of the town were a good deal excited about the location of one from Aurora, in Kane county, to Peru, via. Ottawa. Subscriptions were raised, and one hundred dollars were appropriated from the treasury to defray the expenses of the survey. This road was never constructed, but the interests of the town were afterwards satisfied by the construction of the Aurora Extension, and Chicago and Burlington, crossing the Illinois Central at Mendota.

In August, the National Hotel, owned by Z. Lewis Esq., was destroyed by fire. This was the largest and best building in the town, and was the first serious loss by fire.

In this year, Adam Lerch was appointed Street Commissioner, in place of Thompson who was removed.

In October Hammond and Welch established the "Peru Democrat," a weekly newspaper. It soon took a high rank and became one of the leading and most influential papers in the interior of the State. Thomas W. Welch, the editor of this paper, gave promise of great usefulness in future years. He was a vigorous writer, energetic and industrious, and imparted a degree of vivacity and spirit to his sheet, rarely met with in country newspapers. He was born at Reading, England, and died at Princeton, Illinois, on the 26th September, 1852, aged twenty-nine years.

On the 9th November a resolution passed the Board, authorizing a subscription on the part of the town, of $25,000 towards the capital stock of the Rock Island and Peru Railroad, on condition that the road should make its eastern terminus on section 16.

By the returns of the United States census for 1850 there were 4,500 inhabitants in the town! That this was an error is most manifest. A steady increase of population and dwellings took place from this period to the first of June, 1854, when by a census carefully taken, by one of the citizens, there were only 3,036 inhabitants. A similar increase has been going on until the present time, when there are found to be only 3,652. If such a decrease has taken place where are the tenements vacated? A similar error occurs in the United States census returns of La Salle, the population of which is set down at 3,201. A census, taken by the authority of the town soon after, exhibited 1,100! It is probable that the census taker was contented with the answer of the first man he met, of whom he enquired the amount of population, and that this person happened to be a large lot holder. Generally, in such cases, if the amount stated be divided by two, an approximate result may be obtained.

On the 15th March, 1851, the town of Peru was incorporated as a City. The territory incorporated embraced the South half of Section 16, the South East quarter of Section 17, the North East fractional quarter of Section 20 and all of Section 21 North of the river. The extent of territory embraced in the City, was forty-eight acres less than that in the borough, that part of Section 21 included containing forty-five acres, while the North West fractional quarter of Section 20 excluded contained ninety-three acres.—This territory was divided into two wards. The leading motive in petitioning for this Charter undoubtedly was to enable the City to issue Bonds on account of Rail Road subscriptions.

The first election held under this Charter was held in April, 1851, which resulted in the election of T. D. Brewster, Mayor; Geo. W. Gilson and Jacob S. Miller, Aldermen for the First Ward, and Erasmus Winslow and John Morris, Aldermen for the Second Ward. Whole number of votes 196.—By the provisions of the Charter, the Aldermen were to be elected for two years—two out of the first four retiring at the end of the first year— to be determined by lot. Gilson and Winslow drew the long term. This Council elected Churchill Coffing, Clerk; P. M. Kilduff, Treasurer; F. S. Day, Assessor; A. Roberts, Marshal; Z. Lewis, Street Commissioner; and James Cahill Collector.

The question of issuing Bonds on account of subscription to the Stock of the Rock Island and La Salle Rail Road, (the Charter having been so amended as to continue the road to Chicago,) was submitted to a vote of the people on the 17th May. The vote in the affirmative was unanimous.

Conflicting claims having arisen out of discrepancies between former surveys of the town, a new survey was ordered and established by ordinance, and other measures taken to legalize the act.

On the 22d February, 1852, the Rail Road Charter having been again amended and the Company denominated the Chicago and Rock Island Rail Road Company, the question of an issue of Bonds on account of subscription to its Stock, to the extent of $40,000, including the $25,000 previously authorized, was submitted to a vote of the people. Strenuous exertions had been made to defeat the subscription; and this time there were found to be 16 votes in the negative to 280 in the affirmative. $40,000 of 10 per cent Bonds were issued, and the same amount was subscribed to the Stock of the Road, which during the fall and winter was commenced and vigorously prosecuted.

The certificates of stock thus subscribed for were, by virtue of section 5 of an ordinance passed 12th April, 1852, to remain with the Rock Island Railroad Company in trust, pledged for the payment of the bonds and interest, and convertible into stock at the option of the holder; thus giving him the advantage of any advance of the stock above par, while the City must pocket the loss of any depression below. The interest due on the 1st November was paid by means of a loan authorized by the Council on the 18th October. Interest scrip of an equal amount was issued by the Company, convertible into stock on the completion of the Road.

In the winter, the charter of the Illinois Central Railroad company was granted. The lands, formerly ceded by Congress, were donated to this company, upon the condition that they should build a road from the mouth of the Ohio to the junction of the canal and Illinois river, with branches &c. The same terms were prescribed by Congress in the act of cession. The people of Peru assumed, that by this it was intended that it should terminate at the pier head, where the waters of the canal and river unite. The company proceeded to build the bridge across the river at the mouth of the Little Vermillion, a mile and a-half above. This drew forth a vigorous protest from the City Council which was duly forwarded to the officers of the company, and to the proper Department at Washington. Nothing however came of it, and the company proceeded to complete their works according to their original plan. This gave to the rival City of La Salle still further advantages, by way for facilities of trade, north and south.

On the 5th February, 1850, the Peru and Grandetour Plank Road company was organized, under a charter previously obtained, by the election of T. D. Brewster, J. H. McMillan, William Paul and J. L. McCormick of Peru, Tracy Reeve of Lamoile, F. R. Dutcher of Shelburn, and Solon Cummings of Grandetour, Directors. In September, 1851, so much of the road was completed as justified, under the charter, the collection of tolls. It was afterwards completed as far as Arlington, in Bureau county, and partially constructed to Lamoile. This enterprise was looked upon as promising great advantages, not only to the town, but also to the country through which it passed. The result demonstrated that these expectations were reasonable. The large traffic which passed over it, for a few succeeding years, could not by any possibility have existed without it. It was originally contemplated to finish it to Grandetour, on Rock river, but want of funds delayed the work, until the construction of intersecting lines of Railroads, in a degree, superseded its necessity. The road has since been allowed to run down, and the plank have been removed. The company at present do not pretend to exercise any control over it. For a great portion of the present season, it has been in so bad a condition as to be quite impassable for loaded teams, and nearly so for vehicles of any description. Thus cut off from the trade of the north by bad roads, and of the south by the difficulty in crossing the river and bottom, the only resource that remained to the trading portion of the community, was to trade with each other. In this it is to be hoped they have been as successful as the boys who traded jack-knives with each other all day.

CHAPTER VIII

At an election held on the 5th day of April, 1852, T. D. Brewster was reelected Mayor, John Morris elected Alderman for the First Ward, and C. R. Holmes for the Second. Whole number of votes, 220. The Council elected I. D. Taylor. Clerk; P. M. Kilduff, Treasurer; E. S. Holbrook, Assessor; Richard Lonsbury, Collector and Street commissioner; and Fredrick Schulte, Marshal.

During the Summer, the Cholera again made its appearance, and with increased violence.—From the first settlement of the town to 1849, with the exception of the years 1838 and 1839, when bilious fevers prevailed to some extent, the inhabitants had enjoyed immunity from disease, seldom experienced in new western settlements, or indeed in any other. For the space of one year, no death occurred except from casualty. Even the ague found few, if any subjects. Throughout the summers of 1850 and 1851, cholera continued its ravages in the surrounding towns and country, and visited Peru but slightly. In the early part of the summer of 1852, while La Salle and other contiguous places were scourged, Peru remained healthy. At length it appeared to have spent its material and departed the entire country. Suddenly it reappeared; and while the places previously afflicted remained healthy, Peru was devastated to an extent not surpassed, if equaled, by any place in the United States. The estimated number of victims was from five to six hundred, being about one-sixth of the entire population. It was observed that less panic and excitement were produced than upon its visitation in 1849. But few cases occurred in the two following years; and from that time to the present—1858—the same freedom from disease has prevailed which distinguished its early settlement. Throughout this year operations on the Railroad were pushed forward with great energy.

At an election held on the 4th April, 1853, P. M. Kilduff and H. S. Beebe each received 144 votes for Mayor. Churchill Coffing was elected Alderman for the First Ward, and John L. Coates for the Second Ward. On counting the votes for Mayor, a question arose concerning the validity of a ballot deposited for Beebe. By the statute it is provided that if, upon counting the votes given at any election, two ballots shall be found folded together, attempt at fraud shall be presumed and both ballots thrown out. In this case one piece of paper was found with the name of Beebe printed on it twice. It was decided by the Council that no evidence of attempt at fraud was here presented, that none could by any possibility be thus perpetrated, and that the ballot should be counted as one vote. By this decision a tie existed. The election was then decided by lot, agreeable to the provisions of an ordinance for the case provided, in favor of Beebe. The Council elected J. D. Taylor, Clerk; J. V. H. Judd and R. P. Wright, a board of Health; J. L. Coates, Treasurer; E. S. Holbrook, Assessor; James Cahill, Collector; J. P. Thompson, Marshal; T. E. G. Ransom, Surveyor; and A. F. Powers, Sexton. The place of John Morris becoming vacant by means of his removal from the Ward, J. L. McCormick was elected Alderman in his place. The May interest on the Railroad bonds was provided for in the same manner as on the preceding November.

On the 21st May Beebe resigned as Mayor, and a new election was ordered which resulted in the election of Kilduff by 52 majority, Beebe being again his opponent. Whole number of votes 298.

On the 20th August $5,000 of bonds, bearing ten per cent. interest, were authorized to be issued for the purpose of building a City Hall and for current expenses; and on the 17th September $10,000 of bonds, bearing eight per cent. interest, were authorized to be issued for the same purpose. The $5,000 bonds first authorized were never issued.

In April of this year the Chicago and Rock Island Railroad was opened for traffic and travel to Peru.

The "Peru Weekly Chronicle" was established by J. F. and N. Linton, on the 1st March, and its publication was continued until September, 1856. For ten months during this period, the Messrs. Linton also published a "Daily Chronicle" which was in all respects creditable to them and to the town. About the beginning of this year a serious fire took place on Water street, which destroyed two large three-story stone stores, with most of their contents, one occupied by E. Higgins & Co. as a Hardware store, and the other by J. H. McMillan & Co. as a Dry Goods store.

At an election held on the 26th April, 1854, T. D. Brewster was elected Mayor, Antoine Birkenbuel, Alderman for the First Ward, David Dana for the Second Ward, and John P. Thompson, Police Magistrate. The Council elected Henry Jones, Clerk; Geo. W. Gilson, Treasurer; James Cahill, Collector; Geo. Low, Assessor; W. H. Foot, Marshal; William Lopstater, Street Commissioner; and A. F. Powers, Sexton.

A question arose concerning the validity of this election. By the Constitution it is provided, that at all elections voting shall be by ballot on white paper. In this case ballots were found for Brewster for Mayor, printed or written on paper having a blue tinge—the ordinary blue tinged writing paper. It was contended that this was not white paper within the meaning of the Constitution. The former Mayor refused to surrender the seals and books of the City, and Aldermen Coffing and Coates abstained from the meetings of the Council. The question was carried by mandamus to the Supreme Court and decided in favor of the validity of the election.

No provision was made for the payment of the interest on the Railroad bonds due on the 1st of May, until the 26th August, when a loan for that purpose was authorized. In this, as on former occasions of paying interest on these bonds, a loss of about $300 was sustained by the City which was made up from the general fund. This arose from the depreciation of the interest scrip issued by the company, which did not bear interest, and which was not convertible until the completion of the Road, and from exchange.

In April of this year, the Chicago and Rock Island Railroad was opened to Rock Island, its entire length. No particular improvement in business took place in consequence.

By a census taken on the 1st June, the number of inhabitants was found to be 3,036.

In January, 1855, the new Market House and City Hall was completed. On the 10th February $2,600 of eight per cent. bonds were issued to pay the balance due the contractors.

CHAPTER IX

At an Election held on the 2d April, 1855, Geo. W. Gilson was elected Mayor, R. H. Booth Alderman for the First Ward, and A. L. Shepherd for the Second Ward. The Council elected Henry Jones, Clerk; W. Johnson, Treasurer; J. B. White, Collector; Isaac Abraham, Assessor; Peter Fought and William Wilde, Street Commissioners; G. N. McKinzie, Marshall; Chas. Blanchard, Attorney; T. E. G. Ransom, Surveyor; John Higgins, Health Officer; A. F. Powers, Sexton; and Chas. Love and A. L. Bull, Fire Wardens.

On the 12th April the City indebtedness was ascertained to be as follows:

Bonds issued on account of Railroad	$40,000
Bonds issued on account of Market House	12,600
Scrip outstanding	1,950
Total City indebtedness	$54,550

On the 30th May a further issue of $5,000 eight per cent. bonds was authorized by the Council for current expenses, which were issued and sold for 4,500.

On the 25th July, R. A. Winston was elected Alderman for the Second Ward, in place of Shepherd whose office became vacant by reason of his removal from that Ward.

On the 8th December Gilson resigned as Mayor.

On the 22nd December Ransom resigned as Surveyor, and H. H. Brown was elected in his place.

The "Peru Sentinel," a weekly newspaper, was established by J. L. McCormick and Guy Hulett in August. It was always a Democratic organ, and now having passed under the management of J. F. Meginness Esq., is fighting valiantly for Douglas and against Lecompton.[1]

On the 7th April, 1856, J. L. McCormick was elected Mayor, P. M. Kilduff Alderman for the First Ward, and C. L. Huntoon for the Second Ward. The Council elected M. C. Harmon, Clerk; J. B. White, Treasurer; Chas. Blanchard, Attorney; Henry Jones, Collector; Geo. O. Banks, Assessor; Peter Fought and J. P. Thompson, Street Commissioners; H. H. Brown, Surveyor; W. H. Foot, Marshal.

In the month of May the Round House, belonging to the Chicago and Rock Island Railroad Company, was destroyed by fire.

On the 17th June the question of issuing $20,000 bonds on account of subscription towards the stock of a Bridge Company, chartered for the purpose of building a bridge across the river at the foot of White street, was submitted to a vote of the people. It was decided in the affirmative by a large majority. The bonds have never been issued nor the subscription made — nor the bridge built. Among the appropriations for this year were $575 to H. G. W. Cronise, and $218.50 to Joseph Kelly for damages sustained by the flooding of their stores with water, caused by deficiency in the culverts.

The Railroad Company commenced paying semi-annual dividends on their stock on the 1st of November, 1854, — first dividend four per cent; all after five; and continued doing so until the 1st November, 1856, when an extra dividend of twelve and a-half per cent. payable in stock, was made. From this the City realized $4,825, a portion of which was used in paying off two judgements which had been obtained against the City, and upon which the City Hall had been sold, amounting together to $1,474.50. The balance was used for the payment of outstanding coupons on the various kinds of bonds, and other claims.

On the 7th January another serious loss by fire took place. The Hoffman House, owned by John Hoffman and occupied by P. T. Moore, was destroyed. The building was thoroughly and substantially built, although of wood, and occupied a beautiful site, and was one of the leading institutions of the town. The loss to both owner and occupant was heavy.

On the 26th September, of the same year, an extensive chair, furniture, sash and blind factory, erected through the indomitable energy and perseverance of Geo. B. Willis, was destroyed by fire. Loss about $20,000. The fate of Mr. Willis, who is now beyond the reach of praise or censure, calls for a passing notice. He came to Peru, poor and blind. By his sagacity and energy he so improved his circumstances that he succeeded in building and putting into operation a manufactory which gave employment to about fifty mechanics. The manner in which he conducted this business would have done credit to any person in the possession of all of his senses, but was very remarkable when done by one who suffered under the loss of so important an organ as that of sight. But the load was too heavy for him to carry. He staggered for a time and fell. Disappointment, mortification, anxiety and despondency did their work. The grave holds him. Whose hand was stretched forth to lighten the burden under which he began to reel? Whose voice whispered words of sympathy and hope when discouragement and disaster crowded upon him? Whose was the intelligent self interest that enquired whether a small amount of aid, in money or credit, would not sustain and foster an enterprise which, in its turn, would invigorate every interest in the community?—Whose was the practical sagacity that perceived, that fifty male operatives, with their families and dependants, were of more value in advancing the growth and prosperity of the town than the rows of stately and costly stores, which have for years stood idle and tenantless? Where were the men—generally to be found on every corner—who proclaim that upon manufacturing industry alone must Peru depend for advancement? Ah! When it was perceived that Mr. Willis had undertaken an enterprise to which his energies and means were inadequate, how hands which, had been stretched forth to catch the copious streams of disbursement, slunk into the fathomless depths of pockets! How importunate and inexorable were those cormorants of every petty western community, called by courtesy, "Banks," which had moused into every nook and corner for paper which it was hoped would prove a profitable investment.

In February, 1857, by act of the Legislature, the limits of the City were extended over the whole of Section 16 and 17. This made the superficial area 1462 acres. In the same month an act passed, creating a Recorders Court for the Cities of Peru and La Salle, with jurisdiction over the territory of the Townships of Salisbury and La Salle—six square miles. Churchill Coffing was appointed Judge, and Daniel Evans, Clerk, who entered upon the discharge of their duties.—One term of the Court was held at La Salle. A question arose concerning the constitutionality, of this Court which was taken, by an agreed case, to the Supreme Court, where it was held that it was an Inferior Court; that the Legislature possessed the power only to grant jurisdiction to such Courts over the territory of a single City; that by no implication could the Constitution be construed so as to grant the power to extend it over territory not embraced within city limits; that the whole act must be considered together; that the powers therein granted could not be separated, and if one part was found to be constitutionally objectionable, the whole must fall together; and that therefore the act was unconstitutional and void.

At an election held in April, 1857, John L. McCormick was reelected Mayor and F. W. Schulte was elected Alderman for the First Ward. No election was made in the Second Ward, Erasmus Winslow and I. C. Day each receiving 63 votes. On the 2d May, a new election was called which resulted in each again receiving 63 votes. The question was then decided by lot in favor of Winslow. The Council elected Jno. J. Dowling, Clerk; David Lininger, Assessor; D. O. Sullivan, Collector; H. G. W. Cronise, Treasurer; W. H. Foot, Marshall; William Hackman and Owen Judge, Street

Commissioners; G. D. Ladd, Attorney; Geo. Seebach and J. T. Milling, Health Officers; William Lambach, Surveyor; and A. F. Powers, Sexton. On the 27th May, Ladd resigned as Attorney, and Thomas Halligan was elected in his place.

The Rail Road Company passed the payment of their November dividend and the city also passed the payment of interest on her bonds.

During the latter part of this year a financial hurricane, commencing in the United States, swept over the world. Money vanished from sight as if by the wand of a magician. General health, bounteous crops, and great activity in every branch of industry had prevailed.—Suddenly everything was arrested as though some Titan held his hand upon a brake lever. Peru did not escape the general disaster. Prices of produce became so low that farmers declined to market it, preferring to allow their creditors to wait and suffer the consequences of shattered credit. But few failures, however, took place.—The Banks did not suspend. Nobody failed—nobody ever does fail in Illinois until the Sheriff sells them out or shuts them up.

On the 11th October, the Foundry and Machine Shop of Fitzsimmons and Beebe was destroyed by fire. Loss $16,500—insurance $5,500. This establishment had given employment to some thirty or forty men. Thus another of the industrial establishments of Peru went out. It is a gloomy fact, and by no means promising sign, that with the exception of the stores of E. Higgins & Co., and McMillan & Co., no important establishment, destroyed by fire, has been rebuilt. The blackened walls and foundations of the National Hotel, Hoffman House, Lauber's Cabinet Shop, the Chair Factory and the Foundry and Machine Shop betray the lack of recuperative energies.

At an election held on the 5th of April, 1858, John L. McCormick was again reelected Mayor, and N. Young was elected Alderman for the First Ward, James Cahill for the Second Ward, and P. M. Kilduff, Police Magistrate. The Council elected John J. Dowling, Clerk; H. G. W. Cronise, Treasurer; T. P. Halligan, Attorney; D. O. Sullivan, Collector; Henry Jones, Assessor; P. W. Milander and Owen Judge, Street Commissioners; W. F. Lambach, Surveyor; G. W. Lininger and Bartlett Denny, Fire Wardens; G. W. Lininger Inspector of weights and measures; A. L. Bull, inspector of lumber and wood; W. H. Foot, Marshal; John Scott and Michael Noon, Assistant Marshals; and A. F. Powers Sexton.

On the 7th day of June, the question of issuing $5,000 of ten per cent. bonds, for the purpose of paying the interest over due on the bonds before issued, was submitted to a vote of the people and decided affirmatively by 21 majority.

The Spring of this year was remarkable for heavy and protracted rains. The roads from the 1st May to the 1st July were nearly impassable, and the ground was so saturated as to make cultivation impossible. About the middle of June it ceased raining, and crops which were thought to be ruined came forward with remarkable promise. At this present writing (10th July) every indication exists of a full average crop.

The grain and other produce, which had been kept back on account of low prices in the fall, could not be brought to market in the spring on account of the bad condition of the roads. At this time, however, the streets are crowded with teams, fair prices are paid for produce, debts are being liquidated, the merchants and mechanics are busy and satisfied, and every interest is reviving.

FOOTNOTE:

[1] On the 17th August, this office was destroyed by fire. The building—a three-story brick—in which it was situated, was owned by J. L. McCormick, Esq., and was the first brick building erected in the town. It was built in 1839.

CHAPTER X

We will now examine the present condition and resources of Peru. The following is a table of a census taken 20th August, 1858.

Whole number of inhabitants,	3,652
Under ten years of age,	1,175
Under twenty-one years and over ten years,	561
Over twenty-one years,	1,916
Males,	1,876
Females,	1,776
Born in the United States,	1,841
Born in Germany,	1,118
Born in Ireland,	489
Born in England	87
Born in Scotland,	24
Born in France,	27
Born in Russian Poland,	27
Born in Sweden,	17
Born in British Provinces,	19
Negroes,	3
Born of foreign parents counted as Americans,	869
Number of deaths in 1857,	48

OCCUPATIONS.

Blacksmiths,	30	Farmers,	18
Laborers,	326	Brakemen,	8
Carpenters,	71	Shoemakers,	26
Livery keepers,	4	Constables,	2
Teamsters,	44	Merchants,	44
Machinists,	20	Millers,	5

Moulder,	1	Justices of the Peace,	3
Pattern Makers,	2	Lawyers,	7
Clerks,	35	Porters,	5
Ice Merchants,	5	Barbers,	4
Printers,	9	Tobacconists,	2
Millwrights,	2	Tinners,	13
Masons,	36	Saloon Keepers,	41
Draymen,	5	Tailors,	9
Caulkers,	4	Physicians,	7
Butchers,	13	Lumber Merchants,	5
Grocers,	11	General Business,	15
Saddlers,	7	Civil Engineers,	2
Teachers,	3	Bakers,	4
Gardeners,	5	Jewelers,	3
Painters,	9	Clergymen,	4
Ticket Agent,	1	Coopers,	5
Brewers,	11	Peddlers,	2
Cap Maker,	1	Conductors,	5
Book Keepers,	4	Miners,	32
Lecturer,	1	Tavern Keepers,	7
Wheelwrights,	13	Ship Carpenters,	16
Cigar Makers,	6	Bankers,	2
Cabinet Makers,	6	Brick Makers,	6
Carpet Weaver,	1	Ferrymen,	2
Basket Maker,	1	Pilot,	1
Gun Smith,	1	Musicians,	3
Match Makers,	2	Editors,	3
Boatmen,	8	Druggists,	4
Daguerreian,	1	Rope Maker,	1
Land Agents,	3		

There are seven public schools, four of which are organized under the Union School system. There are six Churches—one Catholic, one Dutch Reformed, one Methodist, one German Methodist, one Congregationalist, and one Episcopal. There are one Lodge of Good Templars, one of Odd Fellows, and one of Masons. The City possesses a commodious Public Hall, erected in a substantial manner of Milwaukie brick, at an expense of over $12,000. It is divided into a Council Chamber, a Public Hall for meetings, lectures, concerts, &c., a room for market stalls, and a calaboose or jail. The warehouses, stores, hotels, and dwellings of the citizens, for solidity of structure and architecture, taste and adornment, are, as a whole, superior to most places of its size, east or west. There are of houses and places of business and industrial occupations as follows:

703	Dwellings and tenements occupied.
15	Dwellings and tenements unoccupied.
4	Dry Goods Stores.
7	Family Groceries and Provision Stores.
2	Wholesale Groceries and Provision Stores (one selling $200,000 per year.)
4	General Merchandise Stores.
3	Stove and Tin Stores.
2	Hardware Stores.
2	Furniture Stores.
1	Leather and Finding Stores.
1	Flour and Feed Stores.
4	Drug and Book Stores.
2	Tobacco Stores.
7	Taverns (one a large and commodious Hotel.)
1	Gun Shop.
4	Bakeries.
3	Harness and Saddle Shops.
6	Shoe Maker Shops.
5	Tailor Shops.
5	Blacksmith and Wagon Maker Shops.
2	Cooper Shops.
4	Milliner Shops.
2	Banks.
3	Private Land Offices.
2	Livery Stables.
40	Lager Beer and Drinking Saloons.
1	Daguerreian.

5	Law Offices.
7	Physicians.
3	Grain and Merchandise Ware Houses, with a united capacity of about 200,000 bushels, besides room for general merchandise.
1	Plow Factory, (employing some 40 hands.)
1	Match Factory.
1	Fanning Mill Factory.
3	Breweries.
1	Flouring Mill.
5	Lumber Yards.
1	Boat Yard.

The central engine house of the Chicago and Rock Island Bail Road is located here. As the engines, with their engineers and firemen, are changed here, many of the employees are domesticated. The quantity of grain purchased direct from the producers, and shipped—exclusive of that purchased by the mill—was 582,641 bushels in 1857, against about 900,000 bushels in 1856. The falling off is attributable to the reluctance of the farmers to market their grain in the fall of the former year, as before mentioned.

A very important branch of business pursued here is the ice trade. About 13,000 tons are annually packed for the southern market, giving employment to about three hundred men, during the Winter and Spring in packing and shipping, and sixty men in Summer and Fall, in building boats and other preparations for the next winter's business. Two steamboats are owned and employed exclusively in the trade.

For some years, attention has been attracted to the Great Central Coal Field of Illinois, the north eastern rim of which underlies the cities of Peru and La Salle. From the earliest settlement of the country the outcrops have been resorted to for fuel. More and more extensive explorations and excavations have, from time to time, been made, excited by the foresight, sagacity and scientific deductions of the pioneer of that interest, Dixwell Lathrop, Esq. In 1855, a thorough examination was made by J. G. Norwood, State Geologist, which demonstrated the existence of three veins or strata, underlying an area of about 500 square miles. These veins vary in thickness, from three and a half to seven feet, the central being the thickest, but the value of the coal increasing with the descent. The existence of another strata, still lower and still better, is presumed, as the alluvial formation, or coal measures, has not yet been passed by boring. A comparison of the analysis of these coals with those of the best Pennsylvania and Ohio bituminous, demonstrated that an open market could be successfully entered in competition. Immediately afterwards, operations in mining were commenced on a more extensive scale and more scientific principles.

Several shafts were sunk and powerful and improved machinery employed. These shafts were sunk in and near La Salle, with one exception, which was in the westerly part of Peru, immediately on the river bank, and on the track of the Chicago and Rock Island Rail Road. The structures, excavations, machinery and outfits of the company operating this shaft are of the most perfect and approved kind. Their facilities for raising are equal to three hundred tons per day. They are working the lower, or best vein—four and a-half feet thick—exclusively, which they have reached at probably its greatest depression, three hundred and forty-six feet below the surface. Analysis and tests, made at many gas works and manufactories, are conclusive in establishing the fact, that no coal has yet been raised, west of Ohio and north of the Ohio river, which is equal to the coal from this shaft, for the amount of steam it will generate, and for its freedom from sulphur and tendency to clinker. What is true of this shaft is true, in a degree, of the coal from the same vein from the shafts at La Salle, the difference being due no doubt to its greater depression.

The importance of this coal field to the interests of Peru and La Salle can scarcely be over estimated. When it is recollected that this is the extreme northern edge of the Illinois coal fields; that the country all north, to the forrest's of northern Wisconsin, is but sparsely supplied with timber, and that growing "small by degrees and beautifully less;" that this country is already interlaced with Railroads, all having a connexion With the Illinois Central, upon which the coal can be "dumped" directly from the mines; that the iron mines of northern Wisconsin are within easy and accessible distance; and that the locality itself possesses extraordinary advantages for manufacturing; its importance can be partially comprehended.

One word as to the advantages for manufacturing. One of the most considerable of these is the cheapness, excellency and unlimited supply of fuel. To this must be added the acknowledged healthiness of the locality and salubrity of climate; and the facilities for drawing supplies and distributing manufactures, by river, canal and rail road, which diverge in every direction, and penetrate a country which, for hundreds of miles, has a greater capacity for production, and consequently for sustaining population, than any other country of the same extent on the surface of the Globe. Laborers, mechanics and artisans can purchase the same degree of comfort here as in Chicago or other commercial and crowded centers, where of necessity rents and provisions must be high, for one third less price. This, it will be perceived, is a very important element to be taken into account. It would seem as if these advantages, combined with other and important ones not enumerated, would soon become so convincing, as to make resistance to the establishment of manufactories much longer impossible.

The present debt of the City of Peru is as follows:

Chicago and Rock Island Rail Road bonds,	40,000
Market House bonds,	12,600
Current expense bonds of 1855,	5,000
Interest bonds voted for in June,	5,000
Outstanding Scrip (about,)	1,000
Total.	$63,600

There is enough uncollected, (or in the officers hands) revenue of the year 1857, which is reliable, to pay all outstanding scrip. The revenue of last year, from all sources, was $8,582,34. The whole amount of taxable property, real and personal, as appears, by the assessment roll, was $1,752,306. It will be seen that the financial condition of the city is by no means desperate. When the rail road shall pay its dividends regularly, if the issue of no more bonds be authorized, and prudence and economy are observed in expenditures, no difficulty will be experienced in meeting all engagements, and gradually reducing the debt.

On reviewing the census and other statistics, connected with the growth and present and prospective condition of the city, there will be found no cause for despondency and discouragement, but much for congratulation and hope. It is true that no such rapid increase of population has taken place as was anticipated, or as has been the case in some other western towns. But there has been no decrease, even temporary. On the contrary, there has been a steady and gradual increase in population, business and wealth, from the recommencement of the work of building the canal in 1843, to the present time. That this increase has been no more rapid, may be accounted for, partially by the influence which the sudden and nearly simultaneous construction of such a net work of rail roads as covers Illinois, exerts upon all interior towns. There are here no mountain barriers to obstruct the construction of a rail road in any direction. With the exception of the Central, they all cross the State from east to west, connecting the Lakes with the Mississippi, and run without much reference to the location of existing towns. The consequence has been, that nearly all the towns upon the river have had their trade temporarily diverted, to a greater or lesser extent; and "prairie towns" have started up, to compete for the trade, at almost every station. These have enjoyed an ephemeral advantage, from their supposed superior healthiness. That this is a mistake, the mortality of Peru, as exhibited by the census table, for one year, 1857,—which is a fair average of every year except those when the cholera prevailed—abundantly shows. That these towns, while they have in no instance wholly stopped the increase of those on the river, but only divided their natural accessions, will shortly react upon their older sisters, and, in their turn, contributed to their advancement and prosperity, is inevitable. This is already manifest in the relation which Peru now occupies in reference to Amboy, Sublette, Mendota, Arlington, Tonica, Wenona, and other towns on the Central, Chicago and Burlington, and Rock Island Rail Roads, none of which had an existence before the roads were projected. That this is, and must continue to be the case, is obvious from the fact, that while she has all the advantages of rail roads which any of them possess, she has in addition the superior facilities which the river and canal afford. That considerable accessions to her population have taken place the present season is proved by the fact, that only fifteen tenements, little and big, are vacant, while over fifty have been erected.—The foreign element in the population, it will be perceived, is quite large. This is the case with all western towns. If, from the number set down in the census tables as "born in the United States," be subtracted the number "born of foreign parents and counted as Americans," there will be left only nine hundred and seventy-two who are Americans by birth and ancestry. But the amalgamation of interest and feeling is so complete, that society moves harmoniously, and the subject of nationality is but little thought of.

It is believed that the mortality, as exhibited by the census table, is unparalleled. It is about one and one third per cent. of the population. This result has been obtained by enquiry in every family and can be relied on as nearly correct. It includes infants and adults, and those who have died by casualty, as well as by disease. It is true that we have not as large a proportion of old persons, whose lives are terminating in their natural order, as in older communities, but it is also true that we have a larger proportion of newly arrived emigrants, whose health is influenced by the fatigue and exposure of protracted voyages and journeys, and by a change of climate and habits. By a comparison with other towns and cities, and with the entire country, it will be perceived that the aggregate mortality is remarkably low. In Boston, according to the report of the Sanitary Commission, for a period of nine years, the average annual mortality was 2,53 per cent; in New York, according to the annual report of the City Inspector in 1853, it was 4,4 per cent; in Philadelphia, according to the report of the Board of Health in 1850, it was 2,29 per cent; in Baltimore, according to the report of the Board of Health in 1850, it was 2,7 per cent; in Charleston, according to the report of the Board of Health in 1850, it was 1,99 per cent; and in the United States in 1850, according to the census tables, it was 1,39. So it will be seen, that the mortality is less, if the year selected be an average one, than it is in either of the above cities, or in the entire country. This comparison, it is honestly believed, presents a fair index to the sanitary condition of the city.

Prominent among the objects which challenge the early and prompt attention of the citizens of Peru, is the subject of a bridge across the river, and a road across the bottom to the bluff, upon which passing shall at all times be practicable. The trade from the north and west which formerly centered here, has been cut off, to a great extent, by the Central, and Chicago and Burlington roads. The most valuable trade which remains is that from the south side of the river. This is sometimes interrupted for months together, as has been the case the present season, leaving merchants to look despondingly upon their crowded shelves, and mechanics to stand idle in their shops. (Most likely they console themselves at Kaiser's—but this is not to be printed.) What means shall be adopted for the accomplishment of this object, is not the present purpose of the writer to enquire. But that some plan should be devised forthwith—always excepting running into debt—is too apparent to admit of argument. There is every reason to hope that the energy, perseverance and financial skill of the present Mayor, John L. McCormick, Esq., who is the devoted and zealous champion of the work, will triumph over all difficulties.

We have now looked at the past and present. What of the future? Will the magnificent pretensions of the "Head of Navigation" dwindle into thin air? Will the metropolitan airs which she assumed and flaunted before the eyes of envious rivals degenerate into the abject cringing of the vanquished and crest fallen braggart? Will the notes of arrogance and defiance which rung out upon the tympanum of an admiring world subside into the moanings and mutterings of imbecility and dotage? Will the hum of trade and industry be hushed in her streets, and be superceded by the fluttering of bats and the hootings of owls? Or will she decline into a quiet suburban appendage of her more fortunate and energetic rival? Or will both places languish in premature decay, while neighboring towns stride onwards in their march to greatness? Will the manufacture of inordinate quantities of gas continue to be necessary to remind the world of their existence? These are questions that must be answered by their own citizens. Certain it is, that if they properly appreciate and energetically grasp the advantages which nature, and a rare combination of external circumstances have placed within their reach, it will be a long time before the antiquarian will have to grope through superincumbent accumulations for evidence of their previous existence. Not merely by the exchange and transhipment of merchandise;

not merely by hotels, lager beer saloons, banking and exchange offices, and houses and places of refreshment and amusement, although they may be all prefixed with the word "city," can the destiny which is their inheritance and birthright be obtained. An intelligent and productive aggregation of bones, sinews and brains must be domesticated upon the spot, whose presence and influence will react, with beneficent results, upon each and every laudable interest and enterprise. No folly or madness can be more extreme, than that of those who think they can sit down with folded arms, and realize dreams of fortunes to be made through enhanced corner lots.

We have glanced at the material and political commencement, progress and prospects of Peru. Let us look at the moral and intellectual phases of her existence.

Among her early settlers were many families of high culture, refinement, social condition, and moral standing. Of these were the families of George B. Martin, H. L. Kinney, S. Lisle Smith, D. J. Townsend, Wm. H. Davis, Fletcher Webster, George W. Holley, Lucius Pearl, H. P. Woodworth, W. B. Burnett, Gen. Ransom &c. Seldom has a new, obscure, western settlement, whose inhabitants were thrown together by chance, gathered so brilliant specimens of eastern intelligence and civilization. There was an under strata, however, which by no means tends to brighten the reminiscence. The idlers, adventurers and vagabonds, who follow public works in new countries, and who congregate at the termination of navigation, made a rendezvous here. Peru, as ought to have been mentioned before, is broken by a precipitous bluff nearly an hundred and fifty feet high. On a narrow strip between this and the river is a single street, upon which most of the stores, warehouses and shops are situated, in the rear of which runs the rail road. — Most of the dwellings are on the bluff, upon a plane inclining towards the river and somewhat broken with ravines. Formerly, as now, the street under the bluff was generally avoided as a residence by the more orderly and quiet citizens. This became the rendezvous of all the congregated rowdies and ruffians. In the night it was almost entirely given up to them. Orgies and revelry were always in order. As this part of the town was, and has continued to be the most visited by strangers, the steamboats landing in front then, and the rail road running through the rear now, the fame of its doings soon spread throughout all the land. The reputation, thus acquired, clung to it; and while no place has had a larger proportion of quiet, orderly, intelligent and refined citizens, no place has had a more unenviable reputation, unless it be the sister town of La Salle. So true is it that the fame of bad deeds travels further and faster than good ones, the writer, when abroad, on informing a stranger that he was from Peru, has observed that stranger involuntarily button up his pockets and move out of the neighborhood. What reason exists for this feeling may be seen from the fact, that during the whole period of the town's history, no riots; no fights, resulting in death or severe bodily injury with one exception, and that among a party none of which ever lived in the town; no robbery; and but few cases of burglary or larceny have occurred. No night police has ever been found necessary except at brief and distant periods.—Schools and churches have received constant attention and liberal encouragement. If the order and external sanctity of an interior New England town do not prevail, the difference in our circumstances, situation and history must be recollected; and that these are not the tests of morality all over the world.

Few among the citizens have yet found leisure to devote themselves to intellectual pursuits, yet it is believed that the clergymen, lawyers, doctors, merchants &c., have exhibited ability and attainments equal to those of their class in other localities.

CHAPTER XI

What ambitious communities these western towns are, to be sure! How they do chirp when they once get their bills through the shell, and while the greater portion yet adheres to their backs! What laughable contortions they make in their efforts to crow, strut and clap their wings! Eastern people must understand that there are no villages in the West. Every aggregation of a half dozen houses, a blacksmith shop and tavern is a city, and their name is Legion. A meeting house and school house—so necessary in the East to constitute a village—are not necessary appendages of a city in the West. Clapboard shells, with their gables to the street, embellished with square battlements to the ridge, are emblazoned with "City Drug Store," "City Saloon," "City Hard Ware Store," &c. There are "first class hotels," too, between which and the rail road depot, gorgeous omnibuses run. When the cars stop, what a din the runners set up of "Metropolitan Hotel," "St. Nicholas," "Reviere House," "St. Charles," &c. Wo, to the unlucky traveler who falls into their clutches. He will find when he comes to settle his bill, that in respect to charges, they are determined to do no discredit to their sea board prototypes.

Here and there, one of these clapboards "cities" emerge into one of brick and stone. Then three, four and five story structures rise like an exhalation. Enormous turrets, bay windows, lofty ceilings, gold and vermillion, marble, iron and gewgaws, without end, without order, without taste, and without regard to adaptability, business or convenience meet the eye on every side. Plate glass windows disclose a profusion of costly and variegated wares and merchandise, and enormous mirrors entice unsophisticated rustics down endless avenues. Turning your eye upwards along these aspiring structures, you behold broken windows and other evidences of dilapidation, denoting the utter uselessness of these lofty creations; and your amazement is no way lessened when you learn, that from twelve to twenty per cent. interest is paid for the money to erect them, secured by trust deeds upon the building itself, upon "out lots," and upon broad acres of "wild lands." Then what palatial residences are reared in the suburbs! Palaces, cottages, temples, pavilions, pagodas and mosques adorn valley and hill top. Domes, steeples, spires, turrets and minarets, gleam in the sun light, peer out of clumps of foliage, and struggle upwards at every unexpected point. Porticos, verandas, observatories, pillars, are here, there, everywhere, in endless profusion.—Tuscan, Doric, Ionic, Corinthian, Composite, Gothic and Yankee architecture are every where attempted, sometimes several of them on the same building, and sometimes all jumbled together.—Around them are close shaven lawns, graveled walks, arbors, climbing vines, summer houses, green houses, and flower plats, all under the care of one, two, three or more Patricks. Within, frescos and gilding, paint and upholstery, marble and porcelain, rose wood and mahogany vie, in their power to please, with magnificent toilets and languid ladies. Carriages, drawn by thousand dollar bays, groomed by blue coated Hibernians, flash upon the vision like the gleam of a meteor. But alas, for the inevitable revulsion! Down on the "business street," in front of premises where deposits are received and ten or fifteen per cent. interest allowed thereon, and exchange is sold on all eastern and European cities, a motley crowd of anxious and excited people—merchants, farmers, mechanics, seamstresses, laundresses, draymen, and laborers—are assembled. What brings them there? Why, Messrs. Dash & Splurge have "suspended"—that's all.

What weazen-faced, moustachioed abortion is that who declares upon "his honaw, the place is almost equal to New Yawk." Why, that's Mr. Hound, junior partner in the eminent firm of De Laine, Brocade & Co., of New York. He is the same individual whose acquaintance we made six or eight months ago, when he visited this locality and was introduced to us as Mr. Drummer. What a capital fellow he was! How bland! How civil! How polite! How he amused us with stories of the splendor and grandeur of the metropolis! How delightfully he sang! What a superb game of billiards he played! How he insisted upon paying for all the Hiedsieck! Who would have expected to see him transformed into the morose, sinister, vindictive looking personage which he now appears? Who would have expected to see his jocund, rounded physiognomy, where a bland and perpetual smile sat enthroned, distorted into a shape as angular as a problem in Euclid? We find, on enquiry, that his present business here is to look after a little matter between his house and one of our leading firms who have also "suspended." He made the acquaintance of this firm on his late visit, took tea at the house of one of them, sang an accompaniment to the piano with the daughters, bade them adieu with his hand on his heart, took a lunch and a "smash" with the "old man" at the "saloon," and left with a long order for silks, calicos, &c. Mr. De Laine, the head of the house, being a little more cautious, consulted the Commercial Agency and found them set down as "reliable—rather extravagant in living, indulge a little in horse racing, but generally attentive to business," and concluded that it was "all right." Hound finds it "aint all right." Mother-in-law owns the house, furniture, horses and carriage; brothers are preferred creditors; clerks and servants are charged with the collection of debts, from the proceeds of which they are to retain arrearages due them for wages; and the landlord has sued out a distress, and home creditors an attachment, which will surely cover every thing, should there be any little flaws in the assignment. Hound comes to the conclusion that he is taken in—sold—done—and that it will not pay even to employ a lawyer in the premises. In fact, his settled conviction is that there is a collusion between all the residents of this portion of the Earth, and that he will not trust any of them again—never.

The writer hopes that he will not be understood as attempting to ridicule western towns, as a whole, or to throw discredit upon western merchants and bankers, as a class. Thriving villages are springing up all over the country, and many towns and cities are great centers of trade, justly depending for their future advancement upon their great advantages for interior communication, upon the matchless wealth of the soil, and upon the enlightened enterprise of their citizens. The merchants, bankers and real estate owners, are, as a class, shrewd and intelligent men, holding their credit and characters sacred and inviolable, and many families live in elegant luxury, fully justified by a permanent and reliable income. Many, here as elsewhere, have been overtaken by the recent monetary calamities, and are suffering from causes which ordinary foresight could not have foreseen.

But whatever may be thought of the advantages offered by the towns of Peru and La Salle—for their destiny is one—for settlement and the investment of capital, there can be no doubt about the inducements presented to farmers and others by the surrounding country. The climate is genial and salubrious, the atmosphere invigorating and free from miasma, and the scenery delightful—alternating from green and billowy swells of prairie, varied by cultivation and improvement, to wild and romantic dells and ravines. Looking eastward up the valley of the Illinois from the observatory on the Chamber's House, no lovelier scene can be presented. The fair and beautiful city of La Salle, joined to her westerly neighbor by continuous streets and structures; the graceful spire of her cathedral rising clear and sharp against the sky; the wooded outline of the Little Vermillion, indicating its sinuous course northward until lost in the blue haze of the distance; the cultivated fields, yellow with waving wheat and oats, or dark with luxuriant corn; the quiet farm houses nestling in their bowers of foliage—homes of those whose "lines have fallen in pleasant places"—the verdant and undulating stretch of prairie bounding the vision as the waters do upon the ocean; the delicate tracery of the Central Rail Road bridge, spanning the broad chasm of the Illinois from bluff to bluff, nearly a mile in length; the silvery thread of the river, now hid by majestic elms and cotton woods, now divided by islands, and now gleaming in sun light, in the far distance; the jagged sand stone ramparts of the southern shore, in some places rearing their perpendicular sides more than an hundred feet above the waters that lave their base; the rounded and cone like tower of Buffalo Rock, rising abrupt and isolated from the valley below—all present a panorama of exceeding beauty and loveliness. Unlike some other landscapes, fair and pleasing to the eye, no deadly or unwholesome exhalations arise from the dank and luxuriant vegetation. The breezes which fan this scene come laden with health and exhilaration, pure as the icy breath of the Arctic Sea. No portion of the United States is more favorable to health than the counties of La Salle, Bureau and Putnam. No means are at hand to enable a positive statement concerning the mortality of these counties to be made, but observation from almost their earliest settlement, and a residence in many other different localities, justify the assertion that it will fall short of most portions of New York, Pennsylvania or New England. It is true that in the early settlement, bilious fevers, of a mild form, rarely resulting in death, prevailed to some extent, as they have in the early settlement of all parts of the country. These have almost entirely disappeared, and have not been succeeded by the more acute forms of disease, as has been the case in other localities. The climate is particularly favorable to recovery from all complaints of a pulmonary character. Consumption—the scourge of New England—hardly exists here.—No doubt but that in a few generations, it will be eradicated from families where it is hereditary. No nepenthe can reconstruct the consumed, vital, human organ; but it is believed that where no considerable inroads have been made, a residence here, with proper precautions, will do much towards staying, if it does not completely baffle the destroyer. It is also true that the country did not escape the ravages of the cholera. What country did? A few elevated, mountainous regions may have enjoyed immunity from that slow, never wearied, implacable traveller, who comes as the wind comes and "bloweth where it listeth, and thou hearest the sounds thereof, and canst not tell whither it cometh, and where it goeth."

Water, pure, clear and cold, is everywhere found trickling through the subformation of gravel, at a depth of from twenty to forty feet. It is generally slightly impregnated with lime, but otherwise holds but little mineral in solution.—Many of the early cases of fever and ague were no doubt to be attributed to the necessity which compelled the settlers to content themselves with the surface water, putrid with decaying vegetable matter, to be found at a short distance below the surface in sloughs and other depressions. Running streams are not infrequent, though not so common, as in hilly and mountainous regions.

The soil. What shall be said of it? The Delta of the Nile, in its original opulence, was not more fertile. It consists of a rich, black, vegetable mould, from one to six feet in depth, resting upon a sub-soil of stiff clay. Its surface has as yet been only scratched. When this shall be expended, the wealth below can be brought to light by the sub-soil plow, an instrument as unfamiliar here as the Koo-i-noor. An intelligent farmer in La Salle County—an old resident—has been experimenting upon a piece of land of a few acres, by planting and harvesting a succession of corn crops, without fertilizers, for a series of years.—As yet he has found no diminution of yield. All the cereals, fruits and esculent roots, adapted to the climate, produce in perfection and abundance.—Winter blight and rust are incident to wheat culture every where, here as well as in other sections; but insects—the grasshopper, army worm, midge and weavel—have never yet made their appearance. The corn crop never fails. In two seasons out of the last twenty, a slight diminution of yield occurred—in one year by protracted rains preserving the esculency of the plant until the season of frost, and in another by drought.—With these exceptions, it has grown and ripened in all its perfection. Of course, crops are "short" with some people always. The Hibernian said that he believed that "if the steamboat never sailed somebody would be left;" so if the frost never comes, somebody's corn will be caught. So, too, the disposition among farmers to complain of short crops is chronic, here as elsewhere. If the statistics, gathered by means of agricultural fairs or otherwise, do not exhibit so large yields per acre, as in places where land is dearer, it must be recollected that cultivation is as yet conducted only in a very rude manner. No application to the soil of materials whereof it is deficient, for the production of certain crops, was ever dreamed of. None of the high cultivation, adopted where that practice is a necessity, is ever resorted to.

No portions of the three counties named are more than ten miles distant from some rail road station, or river, or canal landing, at all of which a cash market is found for every kind of farm produce, and a supply of all kinds of "store goods" is for sale. Leading to these are roads whereon the low places have been turnpiked, and the sloughs and streams bridged, and which, if not so solid and smooth, in wet weather, as those over the flinty or gravelly soil of some portions of the eastern States, are infinitely superior to those corduroy affairs, running through the timbered regions of Ohio, Indiana and Michigan. In dry weather, no McAdam, no pavement, no Imperial causeway is so smooth, so even, so easy, so noiseless as the slightly elastic prairie road bed. Talk of two-forty on the Avenue! A natural prairie road is the paradise of Jehus.

Horses, cattle, hogs—those whales of the prairies—sheep and fowls thrive and are profitable. The high price and great average yield of grain have, of late years, induced farmers, to a great degree, to neglect the dairy. The ruling price of cheese, in the towns, for several years past has been from ten to fifteen cents, and of butter from fifteen to twenty-five cents per pound. Think of that, you dairymen and dairywomen of the Western Reserve, New York and New England!—Cows, grazing through the long summer upon common prairie pasture, and requiring to be fed only through the short winter, and the product of their udders bringing those prices at your doors! Wool growing, too, for the same reason has been neglected. No country offers greater inducements to raise sheep, were it not for the gangs of worthless dogs which most farmers persist in keeping. The carcasses were formerly of but little value. Now the cost of getting them to the great eastern markets is so small, that for that purpose alone their production would be profitable. What delicious lamb, mutton and beef grace our market stalls! How hidden and buried are the kidneys beneath the white, thick, oleaginous covering! How the layers of fat and lean alternate through rib and sirloin! How the rich juices follow the carving knife as it slides, almost of its own weight, through the roasted haunch! Oh, you benighted Vegetarians! Have you no music in your souls? Do no involuntary drops ooze from the caverns of your mouths, as you contemplate the gastronomic treasure, and inhale the rich fragrance which rises like a halo? Oh, you unfortunate denizens of inland eastern towns, who are compelled to essay mastication upon the blue, stringy, tenacious substance which you call butchers meat! What wonder that the dental art flourishes in your vicinity! How would you like to luxuriate upon these grass-fed fatlings of the prairie?

The average estimate of a large number of intelligent farmers is that it costs about thirty-five dollars to raise a colt to the age of four years. For years past the price of a good work colt, at that age, has been one hundred and fifty dollars.

The choice of markets, enjoyed by agriculturists here, is of great advantage. It often happens that the eastern markets are depressed while the southern markets are buoyant, and vice versa.—The location upon the navigable waters of a tributary of the Mississippi, and upon the canal connecting with the Lakes, gives a valuable option to farmers.

One great bug bear of the prairies was formerly the scarcity of timber. The early settlers skirted with their farms and homesteads the borders of timber, and deemed the central parts of the prairie as valueless as an African desert. Experience has shown that these are the most valuable lands, and that no serious inconvenience is felt on account of remoteness from timber. Lumber from Michigan, transported by canal or rail road, is cheaper for fencing than rails, though the timber were at hand. Wire is also used to considerable extent. The abundance, cheapness, contiguity, and excellent quality of the bituminous coal, underlying portions of all three of these counties, obviate all necessity of wood for fuel.

Society is already established and settled, as in older communities. The present race of farmers is as intelligent and enterprising, as a class, as those of the eastern States. The tone of morals and integrity is as high as elsewhere. Schools are everywhere sustained and fostered, and are no where so remote as to render their advantages unavailable. Churches, of all the several Christian denominations, are in reasonable proximity. The price of land varies from five to fifty dollars per acre.

What a difference in the condition of the emigrant farmer now and twenty years ago! Then, having bade good bye to the home and scenes of his childhood, having sold a portion and packed a portion of his household goods, and having exchanged the last sad and faltering salutations with kindred and early and life long friends—each believing that never more on earth should they meet—with wife and children who tore themselves reluctantly from each cherished face and object, he set his face towards the setting sun. A long and tedious journey by land, through primeval forests; over gullied and precipitous roads and paths; across bog, and morass, and fen, and unbridged torrents, and dreary wastes of sand, and scarcely less desolate prairie; with wearied and jaded animals, and lagging and loitering gait; camping out by night and pacing through its long watches, by turns, as sentries; or by canal boat, steamboat, stage and wagon, at length terminated in a bleak and lonely prairie. Miles across an ocean of verdure or a charred and blackened waste, as the season was summer or late autumn, glistened the roof of a settlers cabin; or if this were hidden by the swells of prairie or the convexity of the earth, rose a small, faint column of smoke against the sky. Away on the furthest verge of vision stretched a blue and indistinct thread, like the first glimpse of coastline, as caught from the deck of a vessel at sea. This was the timber which skirted some distant water course. No other object relieved the eye, as it wandered around the circle. The loneliness of ocean—the wearisome expanse of sea and sky—had here its counterpart. The few articles of furniture and clothing, of prime necessity, were hastily unpacked; a rude and uncomfortable domicil was extemporized; a stable, covered with long grass, to shelter a horse and cow, was erected; and a hole was dug in the nearest slough, whence was obtained a limited supply of dirty and impure water. These were the comforts and accessories which welcomed the early emigrant. No running brooks, no trees, no shade, no merry children frolicking to school, no music of Church bells, no decorous and well dressed people, wending their way to the edifice, where the organ's diapason and the solemn chant, in memory, rose with their stately swell, no cheerful faces of neighbors and friends, no kind voices to congratulate in good fortune and console in bad, surrounded and cheered the saddened pilgrims. Soon, fatigue, exposure, privations, bad water, unwholesome diet, repining and discontent brought on the inevitable "ager." Doctors, calomel, quinine, yellow and jaundiced faces, emaciated forms, broken spirits and general misery followed.

Twenty years! Presto, what a change! Rip Van Winkle has awoke! Where stood the lonely hovel, now stands the commodious and comfortable farm house. Orchards, barns, granaries, flowers, luxuriant foliage, pure water, broad fields of grain and grass, lowing herds, good roads, schools, churches, neighbors, friends, cheerful and smiling faces, happiness and contentment have replaced the former surroundings. The poor and dejected emigrant is now the independent possessor of a domain a prince might envy. The disconsolate and almost broken hearted mother who, during long and weary days and nights, in solitude and loneliness, watched and nursed her puny and sickly brood, is now the happy, comely and dignified matron, whose children and grand-children are clustered around her. The friends and kindred with whom she parted so sorrowfully twenty years ago—those of them who are yet spared to earth—are again her neighbors. With them she frequently exchanges visits—from fifty to sixty hours only, at most, being necessary to bring them together. If Old Rip had actually gone to sleep, twenty years ago upon the prairies, upon awaking now, it is opined, his amazement would far exceed that inspired by the neighborhood of the Catskills. Who will now complain of the hardships incident to a removal from the most favored regions to a country, already so far advanced in all that contributes to the comfort, enjoyment and embellishment of life?

On the 6th August the world was astounded by the announcement that the Atlantic Cable was successfully laid. Previous failures had left no hope in the minds of any, even the most sanguine, of such a result. The short, laconic, simple dispatch of Mr. Field—the world renowned projector and master spirit of the work—flew with lightning wings throughout America and fell upon minds, where skepticism for a long time repelled and resisted conviction. Slowly the possibility of its truth gained the ascendency over disbelief and doubt, till at length, the amazing reality of the achievement began to be comprehended. The dispatch to his family of Capt. Hudson, of the United States' Steam Frigate Niagara, from which the cable was laid, was telegraphed over the country and dispelled all doubt. That dispatch, beautiful in its epigrammatic terseness, and sublime in its devout thankfulness and gratitude, will be carried down the coming centuries, as long as the remembrance of the great feat shall survive. "God has been with us! The telegraph cable is laid, without accident, and to Him be all the Glory.

We are all well." In its first efforts at comprehension, the mind utterly fails to grasp and measure the terrible sublimity of Niagara, the awful majesty of Mont Blanc, or the colossal proportions of a vast cathedral, which

> "Defy at first our nature's littleness,
> Till, growing with their growth, we thus dilate
> Our spirits to the size of that they contemplate."

So with the Atlantic Telegraph. The mind is bewildered and baffled when it undertakes to contemplate either the consequences which are to flow from it, or the simple extent of the cable, and the mysterious regions which it traverses.

Far down along the groined and vaulted caverns of the Ocean's bed; along the slimy pathway, strewed with the wrecks of sunken argosies, their treasures darkling in oozy dungeons, and the forms of their once living, breathing, human freight, stark and ghastly in eternal sleep; along rayless and gloomy depths, where silence and solitude, profound and supreme, unending and eternal, encompass, pervade and encircle as with an atmosphere; along submarine alpine peaks, vainly struggling upwards towards the regions of light and warmth; beneath where the storm Fiend rides on the billow's crest, where the tempest howls the hoarse refrain of its anthem, and where sweeps the ice berg, congealed, perhaps, when the morning stars first sang together; stretches a metallic thread no bigger than your finger, uniting lands two thousand miles asunder in bonds of harmony and brotherly love; along which glides a subtle fluid, conveying thought and intelligence—those mysterious emanations of the human brain—and writes them in distant lands as rapidly as they are engendered. A thought is born, and instantly it is stamped upon a human mind two thousand miles away, across the pathless waste of ocean! A human heart beats, and its throb is felt before the blood returns for another circuit. A word is spoken, and it is re-uttered before the sound has died upon the ear of the first speaker! A question is asked, and its answer comes back as the shuttle returns with the woof! A boon is craved, and the heart leaps in exultation as it is granted, or sinks in despair as it is denied, almost as soon as the lips have closed upon its utterance! Stupendous achievement! Is there no limit to the conquests of man over the forces of nature, tangible or invisible? Shall he yet find means, by the clarity of his messengers and the invincibility of his power, to overtake and reclaim the lost and wandering Pleiad, and restore the fugitive to its celestial companions? Shall he go on, step by step, into the shadowy realms of the Impossible, until he shall claim affinity with Supreme

Intelligence? Shall he advance, in the order of progressive creation, until he shall be developed in a being more nearly allied to Ultimate Destiny? Shall the curtains which conceal the arcana of hidden knowledge be gradually drawn aside, and his eye rest, with unflinching gaze, upon the secrets of the Infinite? Thoughts like these crowd upon the brain, stupefied and amazed by the announcement of an event, more wonderful, as a triumph over Nature's obstacles, than was ever proclaimed since the world began.

CHAPTER XII

The writer indulges in the hope that he will be pardoned for the following digression, which, though forming no part of the "History of Peru," is so connected with it as to induce the belief that it will be not altogether uninteresting to its citizens, or to the general reader into whose hands this little book may fall. The present residents, as they turn their eyes over the beautiful State they inhabit, and behold it dotted with towns, cities, and cultivated farms, where the presence of its original inhabitants is as rare as in Europe, where churches, schools and libraries are strewn broadcast over the land, where the arts, embellishments and accessories of high civilization are everywhere present and pervading, and where rail road and telegraph lines intersect in every direction, may find it pleasant, for a few moments, to drop the present and turn their thoughts to the remote past, and briefly follow up the chain of events, in chronological order, to the period which immediately preceded the settlement of the town. A brief notice of events which occurred in the neighborhood, of the surrounding localities, and of the individuals who inhabited them, whose characters were marked with strong and original peculiarities, may also not be uninteresting.

Looking backwards three years before the commencement of this History—twenty-five years ago—we behold the site of Peru occupied as an Indian village. The very spot where is now the residence of the writer is said to have been an Indian burying ground. Northward, the nearest residence of the white man was at Dixon's Ferry, and westward, at Princeton, excepting, perhaps, the Hoskins family near the Bureau. South of the river were some settlements. Along the timber towards Hennepin lived George Ish and Henry Delong; at Cedar Point, Nathaniel Richie; on the bluff, near the old Fort, John Myers; at Bailey's Point, Lewis Bailey, William Seeley, William Groom, Joel Alvord, Asa Holdridge, William Haws, and perhaps a few others; at or near Hennepin, the Willises, Stewarts, Thompsons, Durleys, Donlevys, Shepperds, Zenors and Dents; at Utica, Simon Crosiar; at Ottawa, the Walkers, Browns, Covills, &c.; at Dayton, John Green and William L. Dunnavan; at Indian Creek, the Halls, Davises and Petegrus; and further eastward, the Hollenbecks and Holdermans. At Bloomington, seventy miles distant, was the nearest mill, and thither all the people went to get their corn and wheat ground, until Green built one at Dayton, in 1833 or 1834. As late as 1837, as related by Mrs. Lockwood who then lived with her father, Isaac Manville, at Manville Hollow, in Cedar Creek bottom, two miles south of Peru, when a new mill was erected and it was announced that bolted flour could be obtained on a certain day, the people flocked around it in crowds; and so eager were they to enjoy that luxury, that they employed Mr. Manville's family to bake cakes for them, keeping them thus engaged nearly the whole night, and standing around the kitchen fire—it is not to be supposed that the other apartments were very spacious or numerous—with watering mouths and excited palates, ready to appropriate the delicious pasty, as it came smoking from the pans. Mrs. Lockwood says she was nearly exhausted, and thought the people never would get enough. The frame of this mill was afterwards removed to Peru where it was set up, and is now occupied by Capt. Lewis Goodell as a livery stable. We will now turn our attention nearly two centuries backwards.

The word, Illinois, is a French corruption of Leno. The Indians told the early French settlers that they were Leno-Lenapes—we are men—meaning, we are brave or masculine men, in contradistinction to cowardly or effeminate men. To an imperfect pronunciation of the first word, the French added the termination peculiar to their own language—hence Lenois, and ultimately, by a further corruption, Illinois.

It has been often remarked that the topography and climate of Illinois bear a strong analogy to those of some portions of France. In its primeval condition, there was, in its landscape and atmosphere, the spirit of gay and joyous life, and of soft and luxurious repose which distinguish the Gallic Empire. The broad plains were free from the enervating influence of the Tropics, on the one hand, or the stern and rugged landscape features which nurse the restless Norseman, on the other. These may have been among the reasons which tempted the Frenchman, after their existence had been made known by the explorations of his countrymen, to take up his abode along the streams and groves which diversify them. At any rate, French settlements were made immediately in the footsteps of Marquette, La Salle, La Hontag and other explorers, who carried the Holy Cross of the Church and the Fleurs de Lis of France into these wilds, as early as the reign of the Grande Monarque, Louis XIV. in the latter part of the seventeenth century.—Settlements were made at Peoria, Kaskaskia and Cohokia, to which were transferred the arts, customs, manners, faith and costumes of France, at the period, and where they flourished and were conserved, with very little innovation, until the approach of the American Goth—the rude and semi barbaric pioneer. Little jealousy and few feuds appear to have existed between these intruders and the tawny children of the forest and prairie, by whom they were surrounded, and upon whose hunting grounds they were trespassing. The imposing ceremonies of the Catholic faith, and the simple, frank and conciliatory manners of the strangers charmed the senses and soothed the passions of these children of nature. The French rule in America was, in the main, marked by the absence of those terrible and prolonged conflicts which almost always accompanied Anglo Saxon settlement, in which the amenities of civilized, or even barbaric warfare, were entirely ignored, and each party strove to out do the other in acts of revolting atrocity. The stern, cold hauteur, the rude, coarse insolence, and the grasping, insatiable cupidity of the latter inevitably aroused every demon in the Indian breast. The English colonists knew no arts of Indian conciliation. Their tactics were limited to fire water in advance, and the sword in reserve to avenge the acts of madness excited thereby. The race has not degenerated at all, in these respects, since the marauding Saxon scourged the Baltic shores of Britain. In support of this, witness the efforts of England to force an interdicted and demoralizing commerce upon the passive Chinese; witness her success in saddling the spawn of her aristocracy upon the necks of the subjugated Hindoo and Sepoy, compelling the worshippers of both Vishnu, and Mahomet to bow before crosier and mitre; witness the long and cruel oppression of her Celtic neighbors; witness how we, shoots from the same scion, have carried the bible in our hand and the whisky bottle in the other, while in the rear came the rifle of the backwoodsman to enforce all arguments with the untutored savages; witness how volunteers have rallied around the stars and stripes, and pushed the original possessors of the soil backwards, ever backwards, until a new wave comes rolling from the Pacific coast upon his rear; witness the cruel and inglorious wars—if by that name they may be dignified—in Florida and Oregon, excited by mercenary and unscrupulous jobbers for the sake of a chance of plunder from the National treasury; witness the bullying of and final conflict with the mongrel races of poor, decrepit, imbecile Mexico, whereby the auriferous valleys of California and the sterile wastes of New Mexico were wrested from her nerveless grasp; witness the filibustering forays in Central America; and witness the undisguised lusting after the Gem of the Antilles, and the unblushing announcement made at Ostend, by dignified statesmen, claiming, in the nineteenth century, to be Christians, and representing, not cannibal savages or outlawed pirates, but a people who profess to acknowledge the divine injunction, "do unto others as you would that they should do unto you," and to believe that the command, "thou shalt not steal," is as imperative now as it was in the days of the great Jewish law giver.

But to return to the Acadian settlements of the French in Illinois. The manners and customs of the seventeenth century, as before mentioned, were cherished and conserved by these communities, isolated as they were in the heart of a wilderness continent, until the beginning of the nineteenth century. Passing from French to English rule by the treaty of 1763, they finally came under the jurisdiction of the American Confederation by the treaty of 1783. After the treaty of Ghent in 1814 the restless American pioneer began to make encroachments. The contrast between these two representatives of their respective races, thus meeting face to face in the wilderness, was even more marked and decided than between the same races, separated by the English Channel. The Frenchman represented a by-gone age, softened and subdued by the influences of more than a century's sojourn, in aggregated communities, among the quiet, sylvan glades of le belle terre. The American, originally imbued with the heartless and licentious voluptuousness of the Cavaliers of the times of Charles II. or the morose, ascetic manners of the Commonwealth, was in either case, transformed and remoulded, but with many of his original characteristics yet clinging to him, by more than a century's residence upon a wilderness frontier, where "no pent up Utica confined his powers," where the most unbounded freedom of thought and action were enjoyed, where the wants of nature and the requirements of taste were gratified in the rudest, simplest and most primeval manner, and where, surrounded by the stern and gloomy grandeur of forest life, continual conflict with savages and wild beasts had produced characteristics which, transmitted from one generation to another, had culminated in a character original, unique and interesting. The salient points which distinguished him were unhesitating self reliance; reckless and chivalrous daring; imperious and resistless will; cool and imperturbable self possession; spasmodic and startling energy, contrasted with intermittent, if not habitual indolence; strong, masculine sense, undiluted with any poetry, sentiment or superstition; scorning wilds and strategy, but always prepared to circumvent and baffle them; hospitable to friend or stranger, and ever ready to share his wolf or bear skin, his hog and hominy, his tobacco and whisky, with all comers; to his enemies bold and defiant, but generous and forgiving; to his friends faithful and true, deeming desertion of their fortunes, in trouble or danger, the most aggravated of delinquencies; possessed of physical powers of endurance which mocked privation and fatigue; eye, nerve and brain steady and true in all emergencies; migratory in his habits as a Bedouin Arab; ready, at all times, to drink or fight, run or wrestle; unlettered and untutored as the savage who had been his companion or his foe; and uncouth and repulsive in action, manners and habits as the bear with which he had coped in a hand to paw and knife to fangs conflict.

Thus were the offshoots of the two greatest and most cultivated and refined of modern nations, vis-a-vis, in the heart of the American continent. Soon the song of the voyageur,

> "Such as at home, in the olden time, his fathers before him
> Sang in their Norman orchards and bright Burgundian vineyards,"

as he floated with the stream, or propelled his batteaux against the current, with pole, and line, and oar, and sail, was hushed forever. Soon the panting of the steamer awoke the long silent echos of the bluffs and startled the aquatic fowl from lagoon and bayou. Soon the swelling tide of a more advanced civilization rolled westward over the prairies, and the "common" of the rustic village, upon whose verdant sward and beneath whose branching elms, enamoured swains and blushing maidens,

> "Wearing their Norman caps, and their kirtles of blue, and the ear rings Brought in the olden time from France, and since, as an heirloom, Handed down from mother to child, through long generations,"

had been wont to "trip the light fantastic toe" to rude and simple music, was illumined with the camp fires and whitened with the wagon covers of the Saxon emigrant. Soon the alloted arpents which, in the exercise of "squatter sovereignty," had been appropriated by each family as a home lot, were surveyed, divided, staked and sold, and an embryo city was rising thereon. Soon the quaint and moss covered church, where Vesper, Matin and Mass had erst been said, chanted and sung, gave place to the "meeting house" of another creed and faith.

The early French explorers established a post at Buffalo Rock which, it is believed, was the first attempt at settlement by Europeans, in the valley of the Mississippi. This presumption is supported by the following facts. De Soto, after his two years wandering among the everglades of Florida and the swamps and mountains of what is now Georgia, Alabama and Mississippi, arrived on the bank of the "Great river" in 1541, "but founded no settlement, left no traces, and produced no effects, unless to excite the hostility of the red against the white man." One hundred and thirty-two years later—1673—Marquette passed up the Fox of Wisconsin, across the portage, and down the Wisconsin to the Mississippi, and returned by way of the Illinois. But he, too, according to Joliet, who was his companion, "founded no settlement, and left no traces." These two expeditions contained the only Europeans that ever set foot in the Great Valley until La Salle, five years later, passed down the Illinois. His route was up the

St. Joseph in Michigan, across the portage by the Kankakee, and down that stream to the Illinois, upon the banks of which he made his first halt and built Rock Fort, where he established a Mission and settlement, but which was afterwards abandoned, the inhabitants taking themselves to Fort Crevecour. That Buffalo Rock was the site of Rock Fort is probable from the name, as well as from its superior advantages for such an establishment over any other place in the valley, from the confluence of the Kankakee to Peoria. This supposition is sustained by Perkins, Sparks and Bancroft. A year or two ago, a brass kettle was found in this locality, imbedded in a strata of coal which runs through this singular eminence. It was reported to have been overlaid by a regular seriated, unbroken coal formation; but as this statement is opposed to received geological theories, it is reasonable to suppose that it was deposited by design or accident, in an excavation made by these settlers.

On the 4th of July, 1778, two years after the declaration of Independence, Col. Clark, between whom and Boone the honor of founding Kentucky is divided, with a small band of frontier soldiers, surprised Kaskaskia, then garrisoned by the British, and shortly afterwards made himself master of Cohokia, without bloodshed. He first brought to the inhabitants intelligence of the alliance between the Americans and their former liege, the King of the French, which was received with rapturous enthusiasm, so galling and unwelcome had been the British yoke. Les long Conteaux, as the Kentuckians were called, and les Bostonias, as the Yankees were called were thenceforth welcome.

The attachment which the Indians always manifested towards their great Father of France, in opposition to the British rule, was quickly transferred to the Americans. In October, the House of Burgesses of Virginia erected the country north of the Ohio into the county of Illinois, over which they placed John Todd, of Kentucky, Governor. Two companies, raised in the French settlements, accompanied Clark in his famous expedition against Vincennes. In 1783, the treaty of peace was concluded, by which the western boundary of the enfranchised Colonies was declared to be the Mississippi. In 1784, the North West Territory was ceded by Virginia to the Confederation Congress. In 1787, it was organized by Congress, but no government was established in Illinois until 1790. This consisted of a Governor, three Judges and a Council, who combined executive, judicial and legislative authority. In this year, the county of St. Clair was organized.—From 1783, when the country passed from under British rule, to 1790—a period of seven years—no government of any kind existed in Illinois. In 1809, Illinois, then including what is now Wisconsin, was organized as a first class Territorial Government, the people electing a House of Representatives, and the President and

Senate appointing the Governor and Council. Ninian Edwards was the first Governor and Nathaniel Pope, both of Kentucky, the first Secretary. In 1812, war was declared between the United States and England. Soon followed the surrender of Detroit, by Hull, and the Chicago massacre. At this time no settlement existed in Illinois, north of Alton, except the small French settlement of Peoria. An expedition, in which the present Buchanan candidate for Superintendent of public instruction, John Reynolds, the "Old Ranger," participated, attacked and destroyed an Indian village on the bluff, at the head of Peoria Lake. On the 24th of Dec. 1814, the treaty of Ghent was signed. In July, 1815, a treaty was made at Portage des Sioux, a short distance above the mouth of the Missouri, between the American Commissioners, consisting of Gov. Clark of Missouri, Gov. Edwards of Illinois, and Auguste Chouteau of St. Louis, and the various Indian tribes of the North West, except the Sacks and Foxes, under Keokuk and Black Hawk, who refused to come to the treaty ground. Two years afterwards, at St. Louis, a treaty was made with these tribes, an alleged violation of which led to the Black Hawk war in 1831 and '32. From this time to 1820, emigration poured into Illinois. It was almost entirely from the Southern States, and stopped south of the Sangamon. The population of Illinois was in 1790, about 2000; in 1800, about 3000; in 1810, 12,284; in 1820, 45,000; in 1830, 157,447; in 1840, 478,929; in 1850, 853,317; and in 1855, 1,300,000.

The first Legislature convened at Kaskaskia in 1812. Not a lawyer or attorney is found on the roll of names. Pierre Menard, of the French settlements at Peoria, presided in the Council.—The Legislature of 1817-'18 incorporated the "Illinois Bank of Shawneetown," the "Bank of Cairo" and the "Bank of Edwardsville."—They all became depositories of United States money. The latter failed soon afterwards, by which the Government lost $54,000. The two former failed, but were galvanized into life during the Internal Improvement mania of 1835-'36, and by their subsequent failure contributed to the distress of the people in 1841 and 1842. In 1818, Illinois became a State. Her constitution was not submitted to a vote of the people. Shadrick Bond, of Kaskaskia, was the first Governor and Pierre Menard first Lieutenant Governor. Gov. Bond, at the first session of the State Legislature, recommended the construction of the canal. In 1820-'21 the "State Bank" was incorporated.—The faith of the State was pledged for its issues. It failed and the State made up a deficiency of one hundred thousand dollars which she borrowed of or through a gentleman named Wiggins. This was the famous Wiggins loan and the foundation of the State debt.

The suggestion of the canal was made as early as 1814, in Niles Register. The extract is as follows:

"By the Illinois, it is probable that Buffalo, in New York, may be united with New Orleans by inland navigation, through lakes Erie, Huron and Michigan, and the Illinois, and down that river to the Mississippi. What a route! How stupendous the idea! How dwindles the importance of the artificial canals of Europe!" Many Acts were passed for forwarding this work—one in 1824, one in 1825, one in 1827, one in 1829, but the law, under which the work was actually commenced, was not passed until 1835.

In 1824, the Sangamon river was the northern boundary of settlements. North of the Illinois, the country was occupied by the Sacks and Foxes. As before mentioned, these tribes were not represented at the treaty of Portage des Sioux, but afterwards entered into a treaty at St. Louis.—Another treaty was made with them at Rock Island in 1822, another at Washington in 1824, another at Prairie du Chien in 1825, and another in 1830, by all of which they agreed to move across the Mississippi. Black Hawk, a brave but not a chief, refused to be bound by these treaties, and in 1831, commenced a series of depredations and murders on the scattering settlements on Rock River, but on the appearance of the troops retreated across the Mississippi. In 1832, he recrossed the river with most of the warriors of the tribes, and defeated Maj. Stillman with 175 men at a place about 20 miles above Dixon's Ferry.—Soon 3000 militia were rendezvoused at Fort Science, which stood near where the river sweeps northward from the foot of the bluffs above Peru. These were joined by a detachment from Fort Armstrong, on Rock Island, when the whole proceeded under the command of Gen. Atkinson, on the trail of the Savages. Gen. Scott, with six hundred mounted men and nine companies of artillery, was ordered from the seaboard, but before his arrival the western troops had put a termination to the war. These moved northward, and by a series of actions—one by a detachment under the command of Col. John Dement between Dixon and Galena, one by Gen. Henry near the Blue Mounds in Wisconsin, and one near the mouth of the Wisconsin— dispersed the savages and put an end to Blackhawk's power. Keokuk, the regular chief of the Sacks, had endeavored to dissuade them from the war, but the councils of Black Hawk, his rival, prevailed. The few settlers in La Salle county at this time—supposed to be about one hundred in number— suffered much from the atrocity of the Indians. After the rout of Stillman, the latter separated into small squads for the purpose of murder, pillage and the destruction of property. A party made an incursion upon Indian Creek, a few miles north of Ottawa, where they killed fifteen of the families of Hall, Davis and Petegru, who were all living in one house. The attack was made in the day time by about sixty Indians, who watched the men leave the house to go to their work upon a mill dam close by, when they rushed from their coverts, one portion firing upon the men, while the other entered the house and slaughtered all the women and children, with the exception of two daughters of Mr. Hall. The men, five in number, had time to return the fire of the enemy several times, with probable effect, before they fell. Two of them threw themselves into the creek, but, on reaching the further bank, they were shot. William Davis and John W. Hall, sons of the elder Davis and Hall who were killed, swam down the stream, and baffled the search of their pursuers. Mr. Hall is now living in the vicinity of Peru. John Green, at Dayton, William L. Dunnavan, the Hollenbecks, Holdermans, and all the other settlers in the region of Fox River, were more or less sufferers, and all had to seek refuge in the fort at Ottawa. One man was killed on the Bureau, six or eight miles from Princeton. Some of the present citizens of La Salle county, remember with gratitude the kindly services of Shabanna, a friendly Indian, at present living at Shabanna's Grove, to whose friendly warnings and active interference they owe their own lives and those of their families.

The two Miss Halls—Rachael about seventeen and Silvia about fourteen years of age—were carried captive to the Blue Mounds thence to the Desmoine, where they were purchased by the Winebagoes for three thousand dollars in trinkets, of whom the Government purchased them for five thousand dollars. They were taken down the Desmoine to Keokuk where their uncle, Reason B. Hall, had repaired to receive them. They were in captivity only fifteen days and were, upon the whole, treated with very little rudeness. Their faces were painted upon one side black and upon the other side red and their hair, upon one side, was clipped close to their heads, while upon the other it was suffered to remain long. One day they were ordered to lay themselves down, with their faces to the ground, while above them the warriors brandished their weapons and debated about killing them, their language being partially understood by the captives. It is probable that the circumstances were very favorable to the acquisition of the language. One day, on their march, an Indian's pony stumbled on the brow of a steep hill, when horse and rider went tumbling, one over the other, to the bottom. The younger Miss Hall has since declared that, notwithstanding all the horrors of her situation, she could not help indulging in a ringing shout of laughter. This, so far from prejudicing her with her captors, gained her their favor. Subsequently, a young brave became enamoured with her and, as a consequence, two thousand dollars ransom were insisted upon for her, while only one thousand dollars were demanded for her sister. While on their march, they were allowed only one hours' intercourse with each other during the day, and a squaw took her place between them as they slept at night.—One of them was afterwards married to William Horn and now resides in Missouri, and the other was married to William Munson and resides on Indian Creek, near the place of the massacre.—This account has been frequently given to the writer by different members of the family, and lately by Mrs. Scott, an aunt of the ladies, who at present lives in the town.

During the years 1837 and 1838, large forces of Irish laborers were employed upon the canal. Some time in the winter of these years, one of their characteristic feuds broke out between the Corkonians or Munster men and "Far Downs" or Lienster men at the Sagg, on the upper portion of the work. This gradually spread itself downwards, until in May, a united effort was made on the part of the Corkonians, who were the stronger party, to drive the "bloody Far Downs" from all jobs. A skirmish took place near Marseilles where the latter were worsted. The triumphant party, excited by victory and bad whisky, defying the civil authorities, destroying property, and abusing and maltreating every luckless county Longfort man who came in their way, continued down the line below Ottawa, to the job of Edward Sweeney, who was a Corkonian. Here they were reinforced by his entire force—about two hundred men—and marched, under his leadership, to the extreme western end of the line, at Peru, whence they countermarched, having swept the line from end to end, of all obnoxious fellow laborers, and destroyed many of their shanties. The Sheriff, Alson Woodruff, summoned a posse to quell the disturbance. Word was sent to the Deputy at Peru, Zimri Lewis, late in the afternoon, to raise a party and form a junction with another from Ottawa on the next day. Lewis gathered what forces and arms could be raised in the town and neighborhood during the night, and was ready to march early in the morning. The rioters, some five hundred strong, bivouacked near the "Carey Patch," or "Split Rock" just above the Pecumsogin. In the morning they moved up the line, renewing the excesses of the previous day. All were armed with guns, knives, scythes, picks, and whatever other weapons could be seized. Lewis' forces were joined at La Salle, which then was a mere cluster of laborers shanties, by a reinforcement of Americans and "Far Downs" under the leadership of that veteran contractor, William Byrne, Esq., who was himself a Lienster man, and whose employees were driven from their work. On the way, the Irish portion of the forces were with difficulty restrained from destroying the property and insulting the families of their enemies who were in the mob ahead.—Upon the ridge of table land, near Buffalo Rock, Woodruff, with his posse, met the tumultuous rabble. The former, tolerably well armed, were drawn up to prevent their further advance.—Woodruff ordered them to lay down their arms and submit to the civil authority, warrants having been issued for the arrest of the leaders. This order was answered by a charge from the mob which immediately produced a retreat of the posse. The forces of Lewis and Byrne were at first placed under the command of Capt. Ward B. Burnett, the present Surveyor

General of Kansas, but who soon relinquished the command to Lewis. They moved on rapidly to the place where the party was held, a short distance from which they overtook the enemy. Lewis repeated the demand before made by his superior, and was answered by defiance and their hostile demonstrations, upon which a well directed volley was poured into them, which was immediately followed by a cavalry charge of such of the forces as were mounted. The mob dispersed in every direction. Some threw themselves into the river whither they were pursued, and several were shot in the water. A large number were arrested and marched to Ottawa. Seven were killed, as known at the time, and three others were afterwards found in the grass and buried. Of the posse, now were killed, but Cornelius Lamb, a blacksmith, and John Bracken, a laborer, were severely wounded. This account of the matter can be substantiated by the testimony of many yet living in the vicinity who participated in the affray, and particularly that by Lewis and Byrne, to whom the writer confidently appeals for the general truth of the statement.

On arriving at Ottawa, the prisoners were placed under guard, while their followers and associates hung in groups about the outskirts of the town. Under the Constitution and laws at that time, every Irishman, though he might not have been but six months from the bogs, was a voter. Here, then, was a rich field opened for the demagogues, and the reader may be sure they did not neglect it. Here was democratic raw material which could not be permitted to run to waste.—Sympathizers were

> "Thick as autumnal leaves that strow the brooks
> In Vallombrosa."

Gen. Fry and other aspiring gentlemen commenced harangues, but were speedily cut short by the "boys" who insisted that this was not the entertainment to which they were invited.

The number of Irish, living along the lines of the canal and rail road, for many years, far outnumbered all other residents; but this was the only demonstration against the quiet of the community which, by concerted action, has taken place from that time to the present, if the riots on the Central Rail Road work, on the south bank of the river, be excepted. The excess and violence, in either case, must not be attributed to the Irish residents, as a class. To the conservative influence of the more intelligent portion, rather than to any exhibition of physical power, is the community indebted for the general good order which has prevailed. The learned professions, merchants, farmers and mechanics are largely composed of their class; and many, who came here as poor laborers, are now wealthy men, appreciating, in a degree equal to that of other citizens, the blessings of a government of laws. The writer is fully satisfied, by close observation, that the influence of the Catholic clergy has ever been on the side of order and submission to the laws.

Of the riots on the Central Rail Road the following account is presented.

In December, 1853, a force of about four hundred and fifty men was employed on the embankment and excavations on the south end of the Central Rail Road bridge at La Salle. A misunderstanding existed between the contractor, Albert Story, and the men about wages. The latter had been employed at one dollar and a quarter per day, but the contractor, being unwilling any longer to pay more than one dollar per day, so informed the men and appointed a day—the 15th—when he would pay such as chose to quit work. The men, on their part, alleged that they had been allured from the East by handbills circulated by Story and his associates, announcing that one dollar and a quarter per day would be paid on the job; and that after they had expended all their means to reach the work, the promise was violated, and they were thrown out of employment, except at reduced wages, with families to provide for, at the commencement of winter.

On the day appointed the clerk commenced paying. Soon an error was found in the accounts which was announced to the men, and the business of paying was suspended. This incensed the men, who rushed into the office and declared they would help themselves to their pay. One of them struck Story in the face. During the scuffle, Col. Maynard, a Superintendent of the work and a resident of Chicago, left by the back way to find and take care of Mrs. Story and her children. While he was gone the assailants were forced from the room and the door refastened, when the crowd commenced with axes, picks and shovels to break down the door. One succeeded in entering, when Story, who was armed, asked his clerks whether it was best to shoot. They said, "no, we had better be quiet." Mr. Story, not knowing that Maynard had gone to take care of his wife and children, went by the back way to the house. Finding his wife gone, he started for the stable for a horse on which to leave the place. The men, seeing him, rushed towards the stable, shouting "kill him! kill him! kill him!" and with picks, shovels and stones brutally and almost instantly murdered him, one man striking him with a stone on the head after he was dead. It has been asserted that Story did fire upon the crowd, wounding one man, but this did not clearly appear on the subsequent trials.

The news of the murder soon reached La Salle, and a telegraphic dispatch was sent to Ottawa for Sheriff Thorn, who arrived with a military force about 7 o'clock in the evening. These, with Mayor Campbell, of La Salle, and about one hundred citizens, started for the scene of the murder.—

On arriving at the spot a number of individuals were discovered, scattered over the hills, some of whom were armed, though only a few assumed a threatening attitude. Being fired upon they stopped, and one returned the fire, and received, in return, two balls in his arm, and was then arrested. The Sheriff then visited the different shanties and arrested all, or nearly all, the men he could find, amounting to sixty or seventy, of which some thirty or forty were recognized as participators in the row, though none were of the supposed ringleaders, but these were subsequently arrested. The Sheriff left a portion of his force as a permanent guard; and the work being prosecuted by other parties, the vicinity, through out the winter, bore resemblance to a regular military encampment.

Twelve were indicted as ringleaders in the affray, four of whom, Kren Brennan, James Terry, Michael Terry and Martin Ryan took a change of venue to Kane county, where they were convicted of murder, when a new trial was granted which resulted in a second conviction. By the clemency of Gov. Matteson their punishment was commuted to imprisonment in the penitentiary for life; and among the last of his official acts, a full pardon was granted. The executive interference caused great dissatisfaction, and upon the occasion of the Governor visiting La Salle, he was burnt in effigy. Six were convicted of manslaughter and sentenced to the penitentiary for one year and served out the term. The other two were not found.

On the bluff, near the old fort, and afterwards at Manville Hollow, for many years, there lived an individual whose peculiarities were so strongly marked as to demand a notice in this work.—His name was John Myers, but more familiarly known, among the early settlers, as the "stallion painter." He was a fair specimen of the frontier man—a type of which is attempted to be described in this chapter. In fact, he served as a model for that description. But justice was not done to his moral qualities. His rough garb and uncouth manners concealed a noble and true heart. He was brave, impulsive and generous, and scorned and loathed subterfuge, evasion, and chicanery as only a noble and true heart can. He liked whisky, as all frontier men do, but he seldom lost his bodily or mental equilibrium.—He was never in a condition when all his native coolness and resources would not have been at command in an instant, had he been assailed by any of his old familiar foes, whether man or beast. He was never quarrelsome, even in his cups, but the wronged or weaker party in any conflict, was sure to find in him a champion as chivalrous as ever raised a shield or poised a lance. His exhilaration was generally manifested in yells, such as no human throat ever uttered before. The most ambitious steam whistle might have been envious of his screams. These he called his blessings. He sometimes indulged in songs. Such unearthly notes were never heard out of Pandemonium.

He would have made the fortune of Spalding & Rogers by singing an accompaniment to the calliope. Many of the present citizens of Peru will recollect his vocal performances as he pursued his way homewards across the bottom above the town. On the occasion of the first opening of a court at Ottawa, he went up to witness that novel performance. Having imbibed a few draughts of whisky, and being rather unfamiliar with the etiquette and decorum of courts, he indulged in exercises not very gratifying to judicial dignity or favorable to the progress of business.—Being frequently reprimanded he became somewhat incensed, whereupon he gave vent to his indignation in one of the most remarkable efforts of the lungs that ever electrified a court of Justice. Judges, lawyers and spectators recoiled in dismay, and it is believed that the pins and tenons which confined the roof were seriously strained.

When first known to the writer, he was nearly eighty years of age, yet his step was firm and elastic, his eye bright and lustrous, in the corner of which there lurked an expression of humor and fun, his mind clear and vigorous, and his voice—well, we won't say anything more about that. Born upon the outskirts of civilization in Georgia, he had wandered along the streams and valleys of Tennessee, Kentucky and Southern Illinois, resting from time to time, until advancing settlements crowded him still further into the wilderness.—He was entirely unlettered, though he managed to sign his name, and, as is reported, sometimes to his disadvantage. Notwithstanding this he noticed all the fasts and holy days of the Episcopal Church, a circumstance which indicated his southern origin. His usual dress was a buckskin hunting shirt, breeches and moccasins. In this costume he appeared, by special invitation, at the first ball given in Peru. This was largely composed of ladies and gentlemen, fresh from the saloons and drawing rooms of the eastern cities. As may be supposed, the etiquette and toilets of the assembly produced no little astonishment in the mind of the rough old pioneer. The ladies eagerly sought his hand in the dance, but shrunk back in agony from its vice-like grasp.

Being once more cramped and annoyed by the influx of strangers he left this part of the country in 1839 or 1840, and took up his residence in Southern Missouri, near the Arkansas line. Years and infirmities soon pressed upon him, when he returned to the banks of the Illinois to die. He was buried in the burying ground at Cedar point. The writer has refrained from a notice of his most distinguished exploits, as he finds it prepared to his hand, in a much better manner than he could hope to accomplish, in the September number of Putnam's Magazine. He would say that, in the main, it corresponds with the accounts he has received from the mouth of Mr. Myers himself, and from those who knew him at the time of the events related.

A party of eight or ten Indians, accompanied by Myers, had been out two or three days on a hunting excursion, and were returning, laden with the spoils of the chase, consisting of various kinds of wild fowls, squirrels, raccoons, and buffalo skins. They had used up all their ammunition except a single charge, which was reserved in the rifle of the chief for any emergency or choice game which might present itself on the way home. A river lay in the way, which could be crossed only at one point, without subjecting them to an extra journey of some ten miles round. When they arrived at this point, they suddenly came to a huge panther, which had taken possession of the pass, and like a skilful general, confident of his strong position, seemed determined to hold it. The party retreated a little and stood at bay for a while, and consulted what should be done. Various methods were attempted to decoy or frighten the creature from his position, but in vain. He growled defiance whenever they came in sight, as much as to say, "If you want this stronghold come and take it." The animal appeared to be very powerful and fierce. The trembling Indians hardly dared to come in sight of him, and all the reconnoitering had to be done by Myers. The majority were for retreating as fast as possible, and taking the long journey ten miles round for home, but Myers resolutely resisted. He urged the chief whose rifle was loaded, to march up to the panther, take good aim and shoot him down; promising that the rest of the party would back him up closely with their knives and tomahawks, in case of a mis-fire. But the chief refused; he knew too well the nature and power of the animal. The creature, he contended, was exceedingly hard to kill. Not one shot in twenty, however well aimed, would dispatch him; and if one shot failed, it was a sure death to the shooter, for the infuriated animal would spring upon him in an instant, and tear him to pieces. For similar reasons every Indian in the party declined to hazard a battle with the enemy in any shape.

At last Myers, in a burst of anger and impatience, called them all a set of cowards, and snatching the loaded rifle from the hands of the chief, to the amazement of the whole party, marched deliberately towards the panther. The Indians kept at a cautious distance to watch the result of the fearful battle. Myers walked steadily up to within about two rods of the panther, keeping his eye fixed upon him, while the eyes of the panther flashed fire, and his heavy growl betokened at once the power and firmness of the animal. At about two rods distance, Myers leveled his rifle, took deliberate aim, and fired.—The shot inflicted a heavy wound, but not a fatal one; and the furious animal, maddened with the pain, made but two leaps before he reached his assailant. Myers met him with the butt end of his rifle, and staggered him a little with two or three heavy blows, but the rifle broke, and the animal grappled him, apparently with his full power. The Indians at once gave Myers up for dead, and only thought of making a lively retreat for themselves. Fearful was the struggle between Myers and the panther, but the animal had the best of it at first, for they soon came to the ground, and Myers underneath, suffering under the joint operation of sharp claws and teeth, applied by the most powerful muscles. In falling, however, Myers, whose right hand was at liberty, had drawn a long knife. As soon as they came to the ground, his right arm being free, he made a desperate plunge at the vitals of the animal, and, as good luck would have it, reached his heart.—The loud shrieks of the panther showed that it was his death wound. He quivered convulsively, shook his victim with a spasmodic leap and plunge, then loosened his hold, and fell powerless by his side. Myers, whose wounds were severe but not mortal, rose to his feet, bleeding and much exhausted, but with life and strength to give a grand whoop, which conveyed the news of his victory, to his trembling Indian friends.

They now came up to him with shouting and joy, and so full of admiration that they were almost ready to worship him. They dressed and bound up his wounds, and were now ready to pursue their way home without the least impediment. Before crossing the river, Myers cut off the head of the panther, which he took home with him, and fastened it up by the side of his cabin door, where it remained for years, a memorial of a deed that excited the admiration of the Indians in all that region. From that time forth they gave Myers that name, and always called him the Panther. (The writer has before given the name by which all the old settlers will recognize him.)

Time rolled on, and the Panther continued to occupy his hut in the wilderness, on the banks of the Illinois River, a general favorite among the savages and exercising a great influence over them. At last the tide of white population again overtook him, and he found himself once more surrounded by white neighbors. Still, however, he seemed loth to forsake the noble Illinois, on whose banks he had been so long a fixture, and he held on, forming a sort of connecting line between the white settlers and the Indians.

At length hostilities broke out, which resulted in the memorable Black Hawk war, that spread desolation through that part of the country.—Parties of Indians committed the most wanton and cruel depredations, often murdering old friends and companions, with whom they had long held conversation. The white settlers, for some distance round, flocked to the cabin of the Panther for protection. His cabin was transformed into a sort of garrison, and was filled with more than an hundred men, women and children, who rested almost their only hope of safety on the prowess of the Panther, and his influence over the savages.

At this time a party of about nine hundred of the Iroquois were on the banks of the Illinois, about a mile from the garrison of Myers, and nearly opposite the present town of La Salle.—One day news was brought to the camp of Myers, that his brother-in-law and wife, and their three children, had been cruelly murdered by some of the Indians. The Panther heard the sad news in silence. The eyes of the people were upon him, to see what he would do. Presently they beheld him with a deliberate and determined air, putting himself in battle array. He girdled on his tomahawk and scalping knife, and shouldered his loaded rifle, and, at open mid-day, silently and alone, bent his steps towards the Indian encampment. With a fearless and firm tread, he marched quietly into the midst of the assembly, elevated his rifle at the head of the principal Chief present, and shot him dead on the spot.—He then deliberately severed the head from the trunk, and holding it up by the hair before the awe-struck multitude, he exclaimed, "You have murdered my brother-in-law, his wife and little ones; and now I have murdered your Chief, I am now even with you. But now mind, every one of you that is found here to-morrow morning at sunrise, is a dead Indian!"

All this was accomplished without the least molestation from the Indians. These people are accustomed to regard any remarkable deed of daring as the result of some supernatural agency and doubtless so considered the present incident. Believing their Chief had fallen a victim to some unseen power, they were stupefied with terror, and looked on without a thought of resistance. Myers bore off the head in triumph to his cabin, where he was welcomed by anxious friends, almost as one returning from the dead. The next morning not an Indian was to be found anywhere in the vicinity.

It is probable that the above may be taken with some allowance. There is certainly a mistake about the Indians being Iroquois, and about their being an hundred people garrisoned at Myers' cabin, and probably about their being any there at all. There probably were some people gathered in the fort, close by.

The title to that portion of Peru, called Ninawa, rests upon the following basis. Lyman D. Brewster, as mentioned in the first chapter of this History, held under the Government of the United States. At his demise he bequeathed it to the American Colonization Society. This body, being a mere voluntary association of individuals, having no corporate existence, was incapable of becoming a devisee of real estate. It followed, then, that the property reverted to the heirs-at-law as of an Intestate. From these Theron D. Brewster obtained releases. Some of them, by reason of their minority being incompetent to execute conveyances at the time, have, since arriving at their majority, conveyed their several interests. Mr. Brewster conveyed an undivided two-tenths in section seventeen, and an undivided four-tenths in section twenty to Col. H. L. Kinney, by whom various undivided interests were sold—one to Col. Ward B. Burnett, one to Capt. Richard Philips, of the St. Louis Democrat, one to Hon. Henry Hubbard, of New Hampshire, and one to Hon. Daniel Webster, of the United States of America. Mr. Brewster sold another undivided interest to Penn & Holmes of Montreal, by whom it was conveyed to E. D. Whitney, of Philadelphia. Through some, or all of these parties, the title to all property in Ninawa Addition is derived.

Col. Kinney occupied a very conspicuous position in the incipient stages of the existence of Peru. He emigrated from Bradford county, Penn., in 1838, and commenced making a new farm on the west bank of Spring Creek, working assiduously during the following winter at splitting rails. In 1835, in connection with Capt. Ulysses Spaulding, he built a store where Peru now stands and filled it with goods. Upon the letting of work on the canal, he became a contractor for all that portion below the Little Vermillion, including locks, basin and channel, amounting to nearly a million of dollars. He soon embarked in other speculations and business, and became the most influential and noted man in this part of the State. In 1837 and the early part of 1838, everybody's movements appeared to be regulated by those of Col. Kinney. He was the central Sun from whom all lesser orbs borrowed their light. In 1837, Kinney became disconnected from Spaulding, and was joined by Daniel J. Townsend. A portion of the business was then conducted in the name of Townsend & Kinney. In 1838, their affairs fell into confusion and Kinney left. It was wonderful how many people, in the town and vicinity, were ruined by his failure. Many, who had been brought here from Pennsylvania at his expense, and had lived upon his bounty while here, were suddenly ruined by the treachery and perfidy of their friend, and, as a consequence, were entirely unable to meet their own little engagements.

Col. Kinney, as is well known, was and is a man of indomitable energy, and possessed of a brain fertile with vast schemes and gigantic enterprises. He is said to have rode once to Chicago, a distance of one hundred miles, without leaving his saddle. Gen. Taylor reported him as having moved a command of mounted men, in the Mexican War, one hundred miles in twenty-four hours—a feat, it is believed, without a parallel. His address and manners were captivating in the extreme, and he possessed a sort of magnetic power to bind all who came within the sphere of his influence, to his interests and fortunes. His hospitality and liberality were circumscribed only by the means at his command at the moment, and, as a consequence, parasites clung to him with a tenacity known only to that interesting class.—Two of his sisters still reside in the town, and his venerable father, Simon Kinney, Esq., at Tiskilwa.

Col. Kinney soon afterwards turned up at Corpus Christi, Texas. His career thenceforth has become a portion of the history of that State, of the Mexican War, and of Central America.

Among the motley crowd who were gathered at Peru in 1838 was a man named A. H. Miller. His usual cognomen was "Old Kentuck." He dressed in the full splendor of a five-year-gone-by fashion, wore high top boots of brilliant colors, drawn over his pantaloons, with tassels pendant nearly to the scrupulously polished bottoms, and ruffle shirts which the drippings of frequent potations soon soiled, and was generally superbly mounted, the trappings of his horse being gaudy as those of a Field Marshal. He was of Herculean frame—over six feet in height—and always went armed with a brace of revolvers, one on each side, their hilts protruding ostentatiously in sight, a ponderous Bowie knife down his back, a dagger in his belt, and a pocket pistol in his right breeches-pocket which he christened "little Betsey," and upon which was inscribed, "hark from the tombs"—in short he was a complete moving arsenal. Upon the slightest provocation, he would assume the most belligerent attitude and diabolical frown, set his teeth in menacing rigidity, and fumble among his tools, which sent forth certain ominous little clicks. Many was the eye that quailed and cheek that blanched before this personification of rage and power. At length some of the "boys" bethought themselves of the old adage about barking dogs, and concluded to try his mettle. The result was that he displayed the white feather and turned tails to, as the saying is, amid the jeers and taunts of the by-standers. From that moment his prestige was gone, and ever afterwards he "roared as gently as a sucking dove." Those who had quailed before his wrath took ample revenge by bullying him upon every occasion.

The most noticeable places in the neighborhood are Starved Rock, Deer Park and the Sulphur Springs. The following account of the first of these is from Perkin's Annals.

Starved Rock, near the foot of the rapids of the Illinois, is a perpendicular mass of lime and sand stone washed by the current at its base and elevated one hundred and fifty feet. The diameter of its surface is about one hundred feet, with a slope extending to the adjoining bluff from which alone it is accessible.

Tradition says that after the Illinois Indians had killed Pontiac, the great Indian Chief of the northern Indians made war upon them. A band of the Illinois, in attempting to escape, took shelter on this rock, which they soon made inaccessible to their enemies, and where they were closely besieged. They had secured provisions, but their only resource for water was by letting down vessels with bark ropes to the river. The wily besiegers contrived to come in canoes under the rock and cut off their buckets, by which means the unfortunate Illinois were starved to death. Many years after, their bones were whitening on this summit.

Deer Park is a gorge or ravine, worn by the action of water through the sandstone superstructure, about thirty or forty feet in width, seventy or eighty in depth, and about a quarter of a mile in length. It is entered on a level with the bottom of the Big Vermillion, about four miles from Peru, and can be explored with carriages its entire length. The upper end is enlarged into an amphitheatre, about one hundred feet in diameter, and over arched with projecting sandstone cliffs. In the center of this enlargement bubbles a fountain of cool and refreshing water, whence trickles a crystal rill down the entire length of the gorge. During the sultry days of summer it is a delightful place of resort, and, to use a popular term, is extensively "improved." Its name is supposed to be derived from the practice of the Indians, in driving herds of deer into its mouth, when, having no aperture of escape, they became an easy prey.

The Sulphur Springs are several streams of water, issuing from the crevices of the sand stone rock, on an elevated plateau, rising from the river bottom, not far from midway between Ottawa and Peru. Near them is a fine, commodious Hotel, for the accommodation of visitors. The waters are highly charged with sulphur and other mineral, are quite offensive to the taste of the novice, and are said to posses valuable curative properties. For a more particular analysis of these waters, the reader is referred to the gentleman, yet living in our midst, who enjoyed the advantage of listening to Doctor Harrison's learned disquisition, and who has doubtless treasured much of the lore dragged to light on the memorable occasion referred to in the preceding pages.